JUST THE TICKET

FROM LONDON TO SOFIA AND BACK

KEVIN GORMAN

Schulmeister
Publishing Ltd

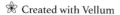

Writing is a form of therapy; sometimes I wonder how all those who do not write, compose or paint can manage to escape the madness, melancholia, the panic and fear which is inherent in a human situation.

— *GRAHAM GREENE*

CONTENTS

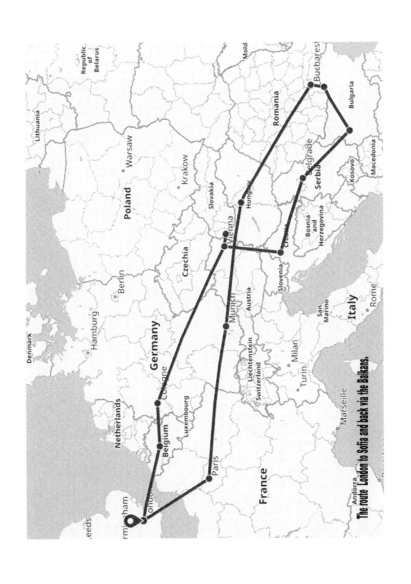

The route **London to Sofia and back via the Balkans.**

PREFACE

In August 2018, I travelled across Central Europe and down to South East Europe and back again by train. I went through ten countries in nine days. The purpose of my trip was to collect facts and information for a non-fiction book; I am working on at the moment. So, it was meant to be a busman's holiday.

Although, I had often thought of taking a long train journey similar to the Trans-Siberian express I could not fit it into my current way of life. Yet, I came back again and again to a deep yearning to travel over a considerable distance. Not that I am a train spotter, an authority on railways, or even a railway basher. I prefer traveling by train as it takes the least effort and can be enjoyable. In fact, compared to flying train travel in Europe is a breeze. You do not have to turn up to the station hours in advance to pass through security. There is no one standing by to go through your bags or request you to remove your shoes then pat you down with a metal detector. It is acceptable to turn up at the last minute, which seems odd these days. Besides, getting on a train is an effortless task. In most occasions, a pleasant experience.

Unlike travelling by plane where you see mostly clouds',

travelling by train is more scenic. During my trip, I spent hours on end gazing at various scenes as the train went through mountain gorges, trundled past rural villages, and fields full of sunflowers. Added to the fact they locate train stations in city Centre's you have the bonus of exploring a particular place before getting your next train. Travelling by train can provide an experience you will remember always and the flexibility of it I think beats flying easily. I am not a great fan of sailing and I have never been on a cruise ship so I cannot compare train travel to sailing.

So why go around Central Europe and South Eastern Europe? Well, I have a fascination with Eastern Europe, which first begun during the late 1980s. I was serving with the Scots Guards in Hohne it was in West Germany, and garrison life was a tad boring.

The British Army of the Rhine (BAOR) garrisons were situated miles away from all the main cities and places. The sole option to escape the humdrum life in a barracks was to own a car. Therefore, in 1991 I bought my first ever car a British Racing Green Mini-Cooper. It was ideal for driving around the well-maintained country roads that surrounded Bergen and Celle. Yet, I wanted to travel further afield to places I had read about or watched in a film. I obtained an old 1950s road map that was divided in two, one part was green, and the other was red. Red side was the erstwhile GDR (German Democratic Republic) aka the DDR or East Germany; the green side was the FRG (Federal Republic of Germany) aka West Germany. It even had the original village names not marked on contemporary maps and it even had the Communist renamed city of Karl-Marx-Stadt, formerly named Chemnitz. They changed it back in 1990. So, it was an excellent map to go exploring the mysterious former DDR.

My initial trip using the map to get across the inner German border (Iron Curtain) took me to a village on the River Elbe. It was not far from Luneburg. There was a bridge marked on the map, and when I arrived it had long since gone. The East Germans or the Russians must have pulled it down after the inner border was erected. So, the only option to get across the Elbe was to use a newly applied financial enterprise of a two-car ferry. Someone local saw a business opportunity after the border opened. It was that trip, which inspired me to explore more of East Germany, particularly concentration camps. I went to the camp at Nordhausen - Mittlebau-Dora at the southern edge of the Hartz Mountains. Then on another trip, I went to Buchenwald near Weimar. The communists preserved the camps for educational purposes and as a grim reminder of fascist brutality.

Places of historical interest were in abundance in the East. I even drove down to Colditz Castle the infamous and supposedly inescapable WW2 Prisoner of War camp. The drive there took me through Magdeburg, Halle, Leipzig, and past the home of the Russian 8th Guards Army, which they still occupied. However, the pièce de résistance was going to Schwerin home of the Russian 2nd Guards Tank Army or rather what was left behind. They were our sworn enemy and the troops we had been training to fight against and protect the West in the event of World War 3. The Cold War was now over and when I got to Schwerin in the autumn of 1991, the Soviet Army were still lingering about their crumbling WW2 era German Army Barracks waiting for the order to withdraw back to the Motherland. I will never forget parking up outside the Sputnik Pub and observing the once mighty Red Army in a miss-match of uniforms. Bartering for basic things like bananas in the street market. They were a sight for sore eyes. Unbeknownst at the time bananas were, in fact, classed as a luxury item and as enemy food. Hardly anybody in the Eastern Bloc had seen a banana never mind eaten one; it was all very surreal! It was the end of an era for the Russians, yet the start of a different one for the Germans.

I went back to Schwerin a few more times during my last two years in Germany. It was a hidden gem of a place with its Schloss and its beautiful lake; it was like traveling back in time, most of it had been untouched since the 1940s.

This fascination I had with Eastern Europe and the Cold War, later led to a master's degree in Intelligence and Security studies, which in turn led me to researching a book about British Military Traitors of the Cold War. This research was the incentive for planning a trip to Central Europe. So, I needed to organise a busman's holiday. Deciding how I would fit it in and work out where I was going to and how I would get there was a wholly different matter.

Inspiration came from two completely diverse writers. The original author was the feminist Rebecca West (Dame Cicely Isabel Fairfield). I had fallen in love with the works of Rebecca West after reading *The Meaning of Treason* and *The New Meaning of Treason*, as part of the research for the Cold War book. She was a wonderful writer and her life is fascinating. Her magnum opus *Black Lamb and Grey Falcon: A journey through Yugoslavia* is compelling. I wanted to go to the Balkans after reading Rebecca West in fact I had to go.

The second author or rather a blogger was Mark Smith and his website The Man in Seat 61. It is the best website on world train travel. I had pored over the website before to research how to get from London to Moscow and back via St Petersburg, so I realised then it was a valuable source of information and intelligence. The way Mark sets out the routes and explains the simplicity of getting from one place to the next made my journey look feasible. Given the way the rail networks from one country to the next are designed I could easily do it in the time I had allocated for it. Going by train was an unequivocal choice!

I would like to think I am a seasoned traveller having gone as far north as Saskatoon in Canada, and as far south as the Falkland Islands. I have been to the Middle East, and North Africa, yet, I have never gone to the Far East such as China. I have travelled around western Europe. However, I had never gone east of Leipzig. Therefore, this journey would be unexplored territory for me. The further I considered it and the more I read about it I needed to go, and then back in March, I put my plan into place. I set myself an objective to go by rail from London to Istanbul and back via the Balkans within 10 days!

JUST THE TICKET

1

THE PLAN

Back in March 2018, I had planned to travel from London to Istanbul and back. After consulting 'Seat 61' on how to accomplish it, my easiest option and by far the cheapest plan was to buy an Interrail Global Pass.

The pass allowed me to travel in thirty countries in Europe within ten days as long as I completed the trip in the same month. I could hop on and hop off as many trains as I wanted within that ten days, it was just the ticket I needed.

Eurail target the Global Pass at the 18 years to 25 years age group. The web is full of YouTube videos and blogs by digital natives who went Interrailling on their gap year or went roaming around Europe for a month or two during their school holidays. I am 47, not as athletic as I was at 25, and I had specially allowed myself ten days to travel around ten countries. So, I had to work out the trip thoroughly. I had to build in my research objectives and list the places I must see and include places that would be nice to see or there was no reason in going. Also, I wanted to have a great time.

So, I reserved my ticket and set a travel date for the 1st of

August. It was a long way off, nevertheless, it allowed me time to organise my objectives and put an itinerary together. Also, you cannot reserve seats until at least one month before you travel; so, going in August gave me ample time to get the route and train timing's right.

My first destination was Budapest. It was requisite I saw this wonderful historic place, which in my point of view is the start point of where west meets east. Moreover, I had no inclination to visit Bucharest or stay anywhere in Romania, but I had to pass through it. So, I had to work out a way of going across Romania then picking up a connection.

The second destination was Sofia; it is the place some say Europe emerged from. Then there was Istanbul that was just the about turn point. Nevertheless, I have a friend who works there so I would meet up with him. On the return it was essential I travelled to Belgrade, as I wished to stay in the renowned Hotel Moskva. Bratislava was my final destination I had to see it. Everything in between well that was just going to be an enigma.

The hardest part was reserving and scheduling trains, which was costlier than the initial ticket. Working out what trains to reserve had to be spot on so I could get off one train and get on another with time to eat and restock up with snacks. I read many online blogs that a lot of the trains had catering cars, but they were not always all open. Another factor I had to add in was places I could get cleaned up in between hotels.

Like all plans, first drafts do not go as imagined, so alter, adjust, then rearrange, and review. I revised the plan repeatedly for about three months. The trouble was I would book one train then a week later I would get an email stating it was cancelled or when I went back to review the itinerary a train timing had changed. This is because some of the countries only run some lines at certain times of the year. Then there were building works taking place at Kapikule on the Turkish border crossing station. Every train I looked at was showing a 24-hour delay between Sofia and Istanbul. So, the only way to get to Istanbul on time was to skip visiting Sofia stay in Bucharest and from there pick up the once a day Bosphorus Express. This was not an option; I had no intention or inclination of stopping in the Romanian capital.

In the end I made an executive decision and dropped Istanbul altogether. I had been to Turkey before and I could see my friend another time. Now I had dropped Istanbul from my plan I had to shuffle all trains around just to get to Sofia on the same day I had previously planned to arrive in Turkey. Otherwise I would have arrived a day early.

Overall, dealing with the route through Bucharest proved to be a test of European Railway timetable management. I could get the 12.45pm from Bucharest to Sofia, which would mean I would need to seek accommodation in Sofia late at night or get off at Russe on the Border at 3pm. If I chose that route then I would have to wait seven-hours to get the overnight train to Sofia, which would mean I arrived at 6.30am. Also, I was not expected to be in Sofia until 2pm. I thought to myself I could easily hang around Russe and Sofia for seven odd hours. So, in the end, I went for the latter option.

Once I had decided on the train route and the timings all fitted, organising the hotels was easy. I used Booking.com and ensured that I could cancel my Hotels at the last minute without paying a cancellation fee. By arranging, well in advance I got some good deals.

The plan was now set. All that remained was my personal administration. I looked at the long-range weather forecast, as this would determine what type of clothing, I needed to take with me. It was necessary to study the customs and traditions of each country I would stay in. The last thing you want to do is to offend a train conductor in the heart of the Carpathian Mountains out of simple insensitivity. For instance, shaking your head up and down in Bulgaria is a 'no' and shaking it from side to side is 'yes' and you do not criticise the history of Hungary in front of a Magyar, they take it very seriously. Call no one East European as they see themselves as Central Europeans. Finally, it was important to consider the internal security situation of each country.

The weather in London had been unusually warm for August so looking at the weather for Central and South East Europe was paramount. There was one alert for storms in Hungary and two extreme warm weather forecasts for Serbia and Croatia all about the time I was going through that region. So, I packed lightweight gear, plenty of T-shirts with no rude words or brand names on them. Two pairs of shorts, one pair of Jeans, a formal shirt, and a waterproof jacket seemed sufficient for what I was going on. Anything else I needed I could get along the way. Walking wise I packed lightweight walking boots and a pair of travel sandals, I did not see the need for formal shoes. The weight of my backpack was light, and when I combined books, rechargeable batteries, special plugs for various devices, water bottles, washing and shaving bag, and a towel, the weight soon ramped up to over 60 lbs.

The Foreign Office provides excellent security information when going abroad; they source it through local knowledge. But there is nobody better than personal contacts who have travelled through or who have had resided in the country you are visiting. One colleague, who in a former life was based in Budapest at the end of the Cold War, gave me some useful language tips and oddly a brief biography of the Hungarian Prime Minister. Another friend warned me to watch out for the people with the heavy coats at the train station in Bucharest, they were the pick-pockets, and another advised me about the man and woman-tailgating trick in the Parisian Metro. It was all useful advice!

So, on the 1 of August 2018 I set off from South West London with my backpack, and great expectations!

2

SANCTUS PANCRATIUS

I t was good to get away from London. I changed jobs the year before and had not had a real break. So, a long holiday was way overdue. Getting on the London underground otherwise known as the 'Tube' early on a Wednesday morning with a backpack is no mean feat. During peak hours, it is crammed with commuters. Everyone squeezes into every inch, and sweats and groans their way to work. As a professional commuter to the City of London, I loathe the Tube during peak hours and prefer to take the bus. But taking the Northern Line is the quickest way to get to North London.

My gateway to Europe begun from the London St Pancras Eurostar terminal, named after the residential area, which was called after Pancratius a venerated 14-year-old Roman citizen. The Roman Emperor Diocletian executed him for being a Christian circa 304 AD. Though, the area around the station is colloquially known as Kings Cross. Once a notorious place frequented by drug users and prostitutes.

Every time I go to St Pancras, it brings back fond recollections of the late 1980s when we had to go through the Army Movements Control Office on the way to Luton Airport to

take the Air Britannia flight to Hannover. Back then the station
was just a provincial station servicing the Midland Main Line,
and it was in a pitiful state. Anyhow, it was good that St Pancras
had a new lease of life as an international train terminal. Per-
sonally, I consider it is an iconic station, with its single-span Iron
roof, which at one stage was the biggest in the world. I am
certain Sir John Betjeman would have approved its restoration.

As an Interrail Global Pass holder, I had to go to the Eurostar
check-in desk rather than stand in the queue to go through the
automated ticket machines. This turned out a far quicker route
through the security checks than it first looked. However, the
passport control queue was very slow. The meandering snake of
tourists getting their passports checked was becoming onerous.
There was no grasp of common sense, some people had to reach
into a suitcase to find their documents. I had mine out in my
hand ready for inspection. Maybe I am intolerant or perhaps it
was just the eagerness to get on my way and start my journey. Either way, it was annoying watching them.

St Pancras to the Gare du Nord is approx. 344 km. and the
Eurostar does it in two-and-a-half hours, unbeknownst at the
time this would be one of my quickest trips. I got in my seat at
10.24am and settled down to have brunch and go over my itinerary. All I could think about was catching my connections or
what I would do if I missed one. Essential to the plan was
making every connection and complete the journey from start to
finish as I had planned it. It was a big gamble; one turn in the
wrong direction or overstaying my welcome in some hostelry
could put the trip out of sync. If the forces of nature made me
miss a connection, I could not do much about that. So, it was
just a matter of maintaining my self-discipline and sticking to
the plan; I had set out for myself.

As the Eurostar moved off from its last stop at Ebbsfleet in
Kent, I settled down and opened my latest book *A Moveable*

Feast by Ernest Hemingway. I had read none of his works before as I seldom read fiction. However, as this was a memoir, I thought it would be a good start to delving into the man himself. It is a small book; I expected it would last until at least Budapest, and it was so good I nearly completed it before I got to Paris. Essentially, it is all about Hemingway's life in Paris after World War I and the lost generation. I will not spoil it as it is a good preface to Hemingway and his specific style of writing. Aside from the book, the journey to Paris was unremarkable as the train passes that quick you notice little.

The Gare du Nord station a familiar site I had been to on many occasions and I know the area well enough to get around. So, there was no reason in taking the Metro or a Taxi to the Gare de l'Est it is within walking distance. Rather than fight the crowds to get to the main entrance I darted out the rear exit of the old station and swung left on to the Rue de Dunkerque. It is a straightforward five-minute downhill walk to the Est station across the Rue La Fayette, which has never changed much since I first went to Paris in the late 1980s. Down the Rue de Fauberg Saint-Denis then you swing left in to the Boulevard de Strasbourg and you cannot miss the beautiful 1850s facade of Paris's gateway to the east.

They had modernised the interior of the original 1850s station since I was last in it. The new boutiques and cafés make it look like an upmarket shopping centre, no surprise it received a Brunel award. Also, it was nice to see Albert Herter's magnificent painting Le Départ de poilus, août 1914 (Departure of the Infantryman 1914) was still there. Although, it is no longer in the Hall des departs it now hangs in the Hall d'Alsace. Herter who was an American artist lost his son (who features in the composition) during the First World War. So, he painted the mural and dedicated it to the people of France, you cannot miss it on your way to the platforms. Compared to the Gare du Nord I much prefer the Est station as it is nowhere near as overcrowded, which makes it simpler to manoeuvre and a lot less strenuous. I popped into the Brassiere Flo just inside the main entrance for a café au lait, and I could not overlook the 'Tarte au Chocolat' so I had a slice of that too. It was delicious. The Flo, was formerly the 'Left Luggage' office, and has the word Consigne cut into the marble above the door, so you cannot miss it. I recommend a visit if you ever depart from the Gare de l'Est.

As I whiled away the hour observing the Parisians and tourists coming and going my mind drifted back to my first time in Paris twenty-six years ago. Strolling through Père Lachaise Cemetery looking for the lead singer of The Doors, Jim Morrison's grave and eating a sandwich au fromage in Saint-Lazare. Not knowing where I was going, and barely knowing a word of French. I reminisced about the coffee bars that sandwich and receiving a favourable exchange rate from Pounds to Francs thinking I was rich.

The Gendarme right outside the Flo suddenly interrupted my reverie. They had stopped a young guy just about to leave the station. Then started to search him when three French Army personnel quickly joined them. I had seen them patrolling the station when I first arrived. The Soldiers where laden with body armour, patrol sacks, radios, and assault rifles. As an old Soldier, I thought it was needless for them to be carrying all that gear, as their reaction to a situation would have slowed them right down. Also, they looked miserable; I do not blame them it was a hot day and safeguarding a railway station was presumably something they never signed up for.

It was sad to see Paris being patrolled by armed Soldiers, but the city had been the victim of several terrorist attacks. We live in a different world now, and it can make people feel safer when there is an armed presence about. The excitement of the stop and search faded, and I looked up at the art deco clock above the bar and saw it was time to head to the Hall des departs and find my platform.

The queue for the train to Munich was disorderly and not properly managed, which was annoying. People were queue hopping left right and centre, which got on my goat. My parents always taught me 'manners cost nothing'. However, worse manners were still to come. A somewhat large African French woman and her son graced with gold chains, watch and rings decided to just barge their way past everyone and get on the carriage first. I got to the door of car 15 and put my foot in the carriage entrance when she nudged me to the one side, or I should say she shoved me out of the way. Both glared at me as if to suggest 'it is my God given right I shall enter this train before you'. I grinned at her and said 'go ahead Missus I am in no rush'. I wished to say something else, but why spoil the start of a wonderful journey on a few curses, besides she would not have understood my Glaswegian accent.

The train to Munich was a French 9577 TGV (Train à Gmain-sails Vitesse) duplex, which is a double-decker train. My first encounter with a duplex train was in Zurich so I knew I would have an enjoyable ride. The TGV is the train that makes sight seeing by rail a relaxing and enjoyable pastime. The direction it was traveling in would give spectacular views of the 'Grand Est' part of France, Lorraine, and the Vosges and the alpine scenery of Augsburg. It covers a distance of approximately 685 km. in fewer than six hours. I had booked a seat by the window for this part of the route, as I perceived I would go by places I had been to in the past, Strasbourg, Karlsruhe, Baden-Baden, Stuttgart, Ulm, and it would bring back fond memories of those places.

After waiting for the ignorant African French Woman and her boy to store their baggage, I located my seat and discovered I was sharing it with another passenger. I had wished I would be alone, as I prefer to have both seats to myself on lengthy trips; it helps me to chill out, stretch my legs out, and enjoy the journey.

There is nothing worse than being wedged into a seat for five hours having to pull in your elbows in so you do not disturb the other passenger. I pointed out to the fellow sitting in the aisle seat I required to get into the window seat. I wasn't sure what nationality he was, so assumed that he was German, so I said 'pardon me I need to get into that seat' and squeezed passed. The chap replied in a soft English voice with a twang. It turns out my fellow passenger was Liam and he was from County Monaghan in the Republic of Ireland. He had lived in Essex, England for about thirty years, nevertheless, you could still hear his Irish accent.

After a brief introduction I found out, he was travelling to Munich. So, he would be sat next to me all the way. I told him I was heading to Budapest and then Bucharest, and he said he was traveling the same way, and his final destination was Istanbul. I thought how fascinating, I asked him 'are you going on the London to Istanbul and back trip then', and he replied 'no I am flying out from Istanbul to Cyprus to see my family'.

It was an odd way of getting to Cyprus by any means, which made it more intriguing. In my mind, I analysed if it was a legit story and if he was legit. I probed a little further, and it arose that he couldn't fly at the same time his family flew to Cyprus. He had gone through ear surgery, which prohibited him from going by air for at least another week. By the time he reached Istanbul, he would be fit to fly. His story did not sound very plausible, yet having had similar ear trouble, I kept an open mind.

As the train moved past, Strasbourg I thought about the summer of 1988. I took a temporary unauthorised leave of absence from the Scots Guards and ended up staying with the French Foreign Legion for a few days at the barracks on the Rue d'Ostende. Then when I saw a motorway sign for Karlsruhe, the vision of my very uncomfortable overnight stopover in a Federal German Police cell came streaming back. Especially, the morning after when the Polizei frogmarched me to a train traveling to Hannover where my Scots Guards colleagues were waiting for me. As I thought about it thirty years later, I wished I had done things differently at a youthful age. Nonetheless, it was all character building stuff and you cannot reverse the past. It has got me to where I am now.

The discussion continued with Liam and we got to the 'what do you do for a living' part, and I discovered he had retired from the NHS, and still worked for them a few days a week. I found out he was a seasoned traveller who had supported his football team all over the world and had been to some far-flung places in his time. The conversation was pleasant, and he was a good sort, and when you put an Irishman and a Scotsman together, it sometimes ends up with alcohol being introduced and this was no exemption. We finished up getting a few cans of Kronenberg together and chattered all the way to Munich.

Having Liam sat next to me made the trip to Bavaria go a lot quicker, but I missed a large portion of the scenery on the way.

Sir John Betjeman, St Pancras Station, London

3

MIDNIGHT TRAIN TO BUDAPEST

I was looking forward to getting off at Munich and spending a few hours in a German bar. I had been to Munich twice and I admire the place a lot. One of the best weekends I spent there was during the Oktoberfest with my mate Charlie. Back in 2001, we got out of London for a long weekend and went to Munich. Unfortunately, a few weeks before we were going England had only beat Germany 5-1 in a qualifying match for the 2002 World Cup. So, I insisted that we both wear as much tartan as possible. I had expected that we might run into bitterness if we pitched up looking and sounding like two Englishmen on the razz. Instead, we turned up at the Wiesn garden looking like two Bay City Rollers fans and we still got knocked back from some of the finest German bier houses. To this day, I still blame the England striker Michael Owen and his hat trick for our harsh treatment. In the end the HofBrau Bier house was exceedingly congenial, and we finished up having a great weekend.

My original idea on arriving in Munich was to find a bar that served traditional German food. Then go to the one and only Supermarket open in the station and stock up on some refreshments and snacks for the lengthy trip to Budapest. I asked Liam what his arrangements where and he replied he was going to look for bar that had been recommended to him. I asked him If I could tag a long as I was looking for the same thing. Liam claimed it was right outside the main entrance to the station and should be simple to locate. When we moved outside, we could not see anything obvious. Although, I spotted probably the biggest rat I have ever seen. Compared to the London rats that used to frequent the grounds of my old Army married quarter in London's Victoria area, this was one was like a Chi wha wha! Anyhow, with no bar in sight and all the 'Schnellimbiss' closing around the station, we decided on having a meal in the station.

Having resided in Germany for five years, I was a huge fan of Bratwurst and Currywurst. So, on staring at the food it was a simple decision, I went straight for the 'Currywurst mit Pommes' and a coke. They shattered my expectations as the waiter presented me with the smallest Currywurst ever, and the pommes tasted like cardboard. However, worse was the omission of curry sauce! It was awful and I do not think for one minute that any self-respecting German would serve a Currywurst without the sauce. That said the waiter could have claimed in his defence it was closing time, and I was just unlucky I got the residues. Maybe, another trip to Munich is called for to compensate for the harm done by the shoddy Currywurst!

The Munich to Budapest Euro Night train otherwise known as the 463 Kalman Imre was scheduled to arrive 23.11pm, but it was running late. As I stood on the platform, I had psychologically prepared myself that I would not be able to puff on my vape machine for the next nine hours. Suddenly, to my complete astonishment I noticed a woman smoking on the platform. I thought to myself smoking on a German platform no way, not with their stringent regulations on health and safety.

But lo-and-behold, there is a specially painted yellow box on the platform for smokers. I had to laugh as the air is no different inside the box to the outside of it. If you stood close enough you would still be passively smoking. Still, I did not care I have never classed vaping as smoking only the law has and now, I could legitimately vape away on the platform until the train appeared.

For this part of the route, I had organised a Gentleman's double compartment on the Kalman Imre, named after the late Hungarian Composer of Operettas. They make the 463 up with five carriages, and not all of them continue to Budapest. On boarding carriage 263, the train steward greeted me, he was a large fellow who looked out of place for his line of work. However, he looked cheerful, and he was courteous. He confirmed my ticket and reservation then showed me to compartment 32. After a brief introduction on how to work the lights and secure the door, he then took my breakfast order and kept my ticket. Once I was settled, he gave me a sharp nod then closed the door. It now allowed me time to sort myself out and get ready for my first night's sleep on-board a Hungarian train.

It was my first time in a couchette-sleeping compartment, and the one in carriage 263 reminded me of the one from the James Bond film *From Russia with Love* when he is on the Orient Express going from Slovenia to Zagreb. I sat back for a minute visualising the part from the movie where James Bond (Sean Connery) battles it out with Captain Nash (Robert Shaw). Then reality kicked in I was not expecting to see any Spectre agents although a visit from a Tatiana Romanova (Daniela Bianchi) lookalike would have been nice. Although, it would have been a squeeze. The double sleeper compartment was perhaps something a Sailor would have been content with. It was not massive, yet it was not too cramped either, it looked cosy though.

On looking around the compartment, I noticed an electrical

plug socket, and a wash-hand basin under the counter. They already made the bed down for sleeping and it came with a fresh clean sheet, blanket, and pillow. So, it was just as well I never brought a sleeping bag; it would have been unnecessary baggage. In addition, there was some complimentary mineral water to drink, presumably because they suggested not drinking the water from the wash-hand basin. Nevertheless, it was better than I was expecting, and it was all part of the experience.

As the Kalman drew out of Munich, I had a profound sense of satisfaction because I felt that this is where my trip started. The last few hours since leaving Paris were just mere bagatelle. Now I was on my way I was excited and enthralled. Oddly enough, it was the same sense I had when I first went into the former DDR, many years before!

Once I had sorted my backpack out, I had a wash in the miniature basin then crawled into the bunk bed. At this stage, the Kalman was gradually driving its way out through the east part of Munich towards Rosenheim. The train was wobbly, and it was mildly rocking me to sleep, moving from side to side, then up and down like a seesaw. I found it a lot easier to work with the motion of the train you drop asleep in no time.

After a few hours of light sleep, I felt the train moving to a stop. Somewhat curious and enthusiastic I got up to look at where I was. Through the blackness, and the mist, I saw the sign for Salzburg. I was now in Austria. I retired back to bed and commanded Morpheus the god of sleep to send me into a deep slumber and wake me up somewhere near Budapest. However, every time the train got to a stop, I felt the desire to get up and look at where I was. It was not until the Kalman reached Linz that the novelty wore off and I plunged far into the delta of sleep.

A sudden jolt that almost knocked me out of the bed inter-rupted my deep sleep. It was so heavy it appeared as if the train was carrying out an emergency stop. I stared up at the window curtain and caught the light showing through, so I looked at my watch and it was 7am. Thanks to Morpheus, I calculated I had about four and a half hours sleep. By now I had presumed that I must be in Hungary or at least near the border. So, I lifted the curtain to look at where I was. The fog masked the view and through the gaps it looked as though I was in the midst of nowhere.

Google Maps showed that the Kalman was in fact crossing the marshlands of the Little Hungarian Plain (Little Alföld). Between the fogs, you could see for miles, and there was no house or town insight. The plain lies in the Gyor-Moson-Sopron County in the western Transdanubia region. It is an area of major ecological and of historical interest. Also, it is densely populated.

The train slowed right down as it travelled past the former border-crossing site at Hegyeshalom, which was formerly a significant meeting place between west and east during the Cold War. They divided this frontier village from the west at first by a minefield, set in areas difficult to patrol, which the Hungarians termed 'műszaki zdr' (Technical barrier). They later erected an electrified high wire fence, with watchtowers. Interestingly, it was in this village on the 2nd of May 1989 when Communism was breaking up that the first physical barrier was torn down. The history is that the Hungarians who perceived what was transpiring and without turning to the Austrians or the separate Eastern Bloc countries pulled down the fence. Someone asked Colonel Balaz Novaki who commanded the Frontier Guards at that time why they told no one, he declared 'nor did we consult our western neighbour when we decided to erect the fence'. It was an audacious step by the Hungarians, but it is in their character. From what I read, they are extremely clever and where miles ahead of everybody else in the Eastern bloc.

As the Kalman went over the Plain, it slowed down for its first major stop in Hungary. Gyor is Hungary's sixth-largest city and has been a vital commercial trading Centre since ancient times. Occupied by the Celts in 500BC and the Romans in 100BC it was previously home to Slavs, Lombards, and Franks until the Magyars settled there in 900AD. Even, Napoleon had stopped there in 1809.

In 1956, Gyor was at the vanguard of the Hungarian uprising. Journalists reporting on the Russian occupation of Hungary used it as a base. Specifically, the CIA (Central Intelligence Agency) funded Radio Free Europe who setup camp in the ironically named Red Star (Royale) Hotel. Subsequently, for a short while later courtesy of the Red Army, it turned into their jail.

Gyor is off the beaten track. However, it is fast attracting tourists owing to its fascinating historical past, porcelain, and vineyards. For me Gyor marked the stage I was in Eastern or Central Europe.

Not long after passing Gyor the train steward came along. He brought me a modest, yet welcoming breakfast with coffee, and informed me that the next station was Budapest.

My bed on the Kalman Imre

Gyor, Hungary

Keleti Station, Budapest

4

PEARL OF THE DANUBE

On getting off the Kalman Imre at Budapest's Keleti pályaudvar East Station, it appeared I had gone back in time to the 1880s. It was a tremendous traditional station that gave me that instant nostalgia of a bygone era. Many of the grand stations of Europe influenced Gyula Rochlitz who designed it and you can see the many distinctive styles at play. It is a fascinating station, with its overarching roof, Karoly Lotz's frescoes gracing the walls and the main facade is 43-meters high.

Statues of James Watt and George Stephenson stand outside representing its relationship with the age of rail and steam. Also, I loved that there was a mystery connected to the station. Underneath the facades Clock, (formerly decorated by a Soviet Red Star) stand four figures a 'Spinner Lady' representing light industry, a 'Picker Lady' representing agriculture, a 'Merchant' representing commerce and a 'Miner' representing heavy industry all erected in 2003. The originals disappeared one night in 1935 and no one noticed or heard anything. Apparently, even to this day, no one knows anything about their disappearance?

I met up with Liam as he left his couchette. As we were on the same train travelling to Bucharest that night, we split a left luggage locker to secure our gear. In need of small change for the locker, I needed to exchange a 50 Forint note. I went into the newsagents next to the luggage room and asked the lady if she could change the note. She refused point blank to help; I thought well I am not buying anything from you. Luckily, a young female station attendant saw my predicament and stepped in and helped me.

It was a good idea to stash the kit as I had planned to go off, do things, and look at places that would have made carrying a backpack around difficult. Moreover, my arrangements did not comprise having someone else coming along with me. Therefore, I proposed to Liam that we meet up on the station platform about 5.30pm and have dinner at the stations Boross Etterem Restaurant.

Budapest's Metro system is right under the main station and it is straightforward to navigate. Likewise, all the ticket machines have English translations making it clear to get a ticket. Although, unlike London where you pay to enter different zones in Budapest you pay for the time your journey takes. However, I was uncertain how long it would take for me to get to my first station, all I knew was that it was on the Buda part of Budapest. Therefore, I chanced it and picked up a fifteen-minute one-way ticket on the M2 line heading north to Ors vser tere.

I got off at Batthyány tér, which is in the heart of Watertown on the Buda side of the city. As you come out of the Metro station, right away you face the view straight across the Danube to the Parliament buildings. Also, you get a great panoramic view of the river and all the tourist boats cruising up and down this magnificent waterway; it was stunning! It is no wonder why they call Budapest the 'Pearl of the Danube'. Anyhow, I was not there to stare at boats I was looking for a building on the Fo utca called BV Gyorskocsi.

Once I had absorbed the view of the Danube, I found the Fo utca outside of the Jesuit Saint Anna Church. After walking for about five minutes, I found the Gyorskocsi building. To be honest, you could not miss this intimidating building. It looks like a fortress probably because it is the epicenter of Hungary's legal and criminal system. It was once a Gestapo Prison and the Ministry of Interior during the Communist era. Today the place houses the Hungarian Prison system, Military Attorney, Military Court system, and their Special Criminal Investigation department. However, I was not looking to pay homage to such a dreadful place. The real building, I was looking was straight across the road from it.

I thought I had stepped back in time when I got off at Keleti station, however I was taken back even further when I went into Kiraly Baths. I had read a lot about the Hungarian geothermal spas and having had a Turkish bath in the 600-year-old Sefa Hammam in Antalya, Turkey; I thought it would be rude not to try out the Kiraly Baths. They call the Budapest Turkish baths ilidzas and are actual warm thermal spring baths with natural hot waters pumped into octagonal pools, somewhat different to a Hammam. Excuse the pun, for a history buff, Kiraly was soaking in history. I believe it is the oldest, medieval Turkish bath still standing in Hungary. According to a local guide it was built in 1565 by Arslan the ruling Ottoman Pasha of Buda. And, his successor Sokoli Mustafa, another Pasha of Buda who was also responsible for the building of several other Turkish baths in Buda completed it. After the Ottoman's left Hungary, the wealthy Konig family of Buda purchased the Bath. They converted it to its current state, whilst preserving many characteristics of its Ottoman past, especially the octagon dome over the main pool.

They know Budapest as the 'City of Baths', and there are far more elegant baths than Kiraly, but I wanted the feel of an old one and here it was, magnificently old, and full of history. Even the modern part felt as though I was walking back in time. It resembled a 1920s sanatorium, probably because the bath is in fact now a Government owned institution. Its previous political ownership was clear in some German and Russian signs I saw. Despite its dated decor, and everyone being dressed in white, you could sense that it was a place of wellness. Having spent nine-hours cooped up on the Kalman Imre my muscles were a tad tired and I had an ache in my neck from the bunk bed so I was looking forward to therapy that would hopefully dispel the pains I was carrying around.

Before leaving for the journey I had been trying to learn a little Hungarian. I think it is important these days you at least attempt to say something in the local language, even if it is just a simple greeting. To be honest, I was struggling to remember some essential words taught by my colleague who I suspected had worked there under diplomatic cover back in the day. Anyway, I tried out the Hungarian I remembered on the Kiraly receptionist and she smiled so I guess I said something right, but I soon reverted to English.

Hungarian has 44 characters in its alphabet, so it is definitely not the easiest language to learn in a short space of time. Luckily, the receptionist spoke a little English. I asked her how long one could stay for and she said If I purchased a daily ticket, I could stay all day if I wanted. So, I handed over 2,500 Forint and a very large refundable deposit for a towel. It was great value for money the equivalent of seven pounds sterling. For the same treatment in the UK; I would have expected to pay thirty pounds or more. Although, I was not planning in staying any more than two hours, it was still great value. The receptionist sorted me out with a towel and a magnetic wristband you used to open and close the locker with. She then directed me upstairs to the changing rooms.

Upstairs in the changing area they still had the old personal booths you can hire for the day if you want privacy. However, the changing room was good enough, it was immaculately clean. I changed into my swimming shorts and followed the signs to the thermal bath down an old winding staircase to a world that definitely takes you back to the 16thcentury, and it smells like it too. The strange smell you encounter is like rotten eggs, yet it is not off-putting. The smell comes from a combination of the hot spring water, magnesium, calcium, sulphur, hydrogen-carbonate, and sodium with fluoride ions. Kiraly baths in fact receives its hot geothermal spring water from the older Lukacs baths situated directly up the road. You can sit right under the tap that pumps it in and get blasted by this natural hot water.

It felt amazing to sit in a 400 hundred-year-old bath, look up at the light coming in from the dome ceiling, and experience the culture of Ottoman bathing.

It was a weekday so there was a mix of people milling about the place. Some elderly and some young, and the good part was it was not packed. If you have never been in a thermal spa before, the concept is to visit the various baths in a sequence. That way you get all the curative aids. I started with the 26°C plunge pool that put my frame into shock, then I plunged into the main octagonal 36°C bath followed by an even hotter 40°C bath. After completing that round, you can feel your veins popping and the aches and pains disappearing. I continued around and around for about 90 minutes. Later, I went for a Jacuzzi for the final half an hour.

After two hours, I went back to the changing rooms feeling totally rejuvenated. On the way out, I had to go via the masseuse office to hand back the towel and get my deposit back. For a place of wellbeing, even cleanliness, there was this overwhelming stench of body odour coming from the masseuse that caused me to cough. I thought how could anybody work in a place like this and smell like that? Anyway, I surfaced on the Fo utca feeling exhilarated and ready to explore the murkier face of Budapest.

They named Andrassy Avenue after Prime Minister Gyula Andrassy it is an elegantly designed 2.5 km tree-lined boulevard that stretches from St Stephen's basilica to Heroes Square. I never knew it was a UNESCO World Heritage Site until I started writing this book. Moreover, I did not know that streets or roads could have such a prestige. But when you walk down Andrassy, you can understand why. It has luxury shops on either side with stately old homes, trams go up and down it and you can relax and watch life pass by on one of the many benches planted along it. Also, it has a very interesting history attached to it. They have renamed it three times since it was constructed. In 1950 the Communists called it 'Stalin Street'. During the 1956 uprising it was renamed 'The Avenue of the Hungarian Youth'. After, the Communists got back in they renamed it to the 'Peoples Republic Street', and when reforms took place in 1989, it was given its original name back.

There are some famous sights on the Avenue, and one of them is Franz Liszt's house, above the old music academy. However, right across the way is number 60 Andrassy. Its grey façade hides a dreadful past remembered by Hungarians to this day. During the war, they knew it as the 'House of Loyalty', which housed the dreadful Pro-Nazi Hungarian Arrow Cross Party. Between 1945 and 1956, it was the headquarters of the infamous Secret Police the AVO and its replacement the AVH, and during the regime of these two organisations, it became known as the 'Terror Haza' (House of Terror) or 'House of Dread'. Now it is a museum and you will understand how it got its infamous name if you visit it. It is a particularly well put together museum and the going down in the lift to the cellar part, which is the ultimate part of the tour was a humbling experience for me. I won't spoil it go and visit it if your ever in Budapest.

After the education of 60 Andrassy I headed towards Brudern House on Ferenciek Square, which houses the formerly elegant PárizsiUdvar (Parisian Court) distinguished for its style. But more interestingly for me, it was a film location in John le Carré's *Tinker Tailor Soldier Spy*. They used it in the scene where the character Jim Prideaux meets a Hungarian General who is considering defecting to the west. Prideaux got shot and hauled off to Moscow. No doubt if it had been an actual situation, he would have finished up in the basement of 60 Andrassy. However, the former shopping Centre is now closed. Apparently, it will reopen as a Hyatt Hotel, which I hope will retain its Art Déco architecture.

Now the sightseeing was over I headed back towards Andrassy to get on the original underground system, which is not the same as the Metro. The underground or Mı line was built between 1894 and 1896 and opened by the Emperor Franz Joseph whose nephew the Archduke Franz Ferdinand was assassinated in Sarajevo 1914. The line is one of the oldest underground transport systems in the world and if you go on it, you will feel as if it has transported you back to the 1900s.

By the time I had found my way back to Keleti it was nearly 5ish and time to meet up with Liam and get something to eat before we got the overnight train to Bucharest.

I had an intense sense of déjà vu as I stepped into the Boross Etterem restaurant at Keleti. I guess it was just the style of the place it looked familiar and similar to some of the old established restaurants I had been in London. Gyula Rochlitz no doubt had styled it on other European restaurants he had dined in. So, I was not surprised it looked familiar. It had that 19th-

Century charm, yet it direly needed a face-lift. However, it was far from unpleasant, it still had a good deal of character left in it.

I selected a table on the terrace facing the platform and the waiter came over wearing a traditional waiter's uniform, with the white shirt, black waistcoat, and bowtie. Also, he was carrying the proverbial tray and white cloth. He handed me a menu, in Hungarian and English, which was convenient, as I definitely cannot read Hungarian.

I had dreamed about eating some traditional Goulash whilst I was in Budapest as I had eaten it as a child. My late Mother's neighbour in Germany was Hungarian, and she had taught my Mum the correct way to prepare it. So, it was a constant dish growing up in Glasgow. However, as I flipped through the menu, I spotted Schnitzel, one of my favourite all time foods, so I elected for that and a glass of beer. Liam went for the Goulash and affirmed that it was good. Maybe the next time I am in Budapest I will try it. I had read a few horrors stories about tourists being ripped off in the Boross, yet my experience was the exact opposite; the waiters were good, and the cuisine was great, and the cost was indeed better. It is unquestionably a place to call on if you are waiting on a train at Keleti.

The view from Batthyany ter, Budapest

Kiraly Baths, Budapest

5

TRANSYLVANIA

I had that sense of dread and excitement come over me all at the same time as the Euro Night Train 473 otherwise known as the 'Ister' (Ister the ancient Latin name for the Danube) trundled into Keleti Station. The dread was from the thought of being confined to a train for the next sixteen hours. However, I was excited by knowing I was about to travel across the Pannonian Plain into the Carpathian Basin and through Transylvania. It is one of the oldest and wildest regions in South Eastern Europe. An area that still have Brown Bears and Wolves roaming around the mountains and forests. Also, it is the historical home of Vlad the Impaler aka Dracula.

As this was one of the longest routes on my journey, I booked a Gentleman's double sleeper. The thought of sharing a compartment in 3rd Class for sixteen hours was out of the question. I wanted to make it as comfortable as possible.

The steward on the Ister was a little squat fellow who had a sincere expression on his face. He never grinned as he greeted the passengers on entering the train. Unlike the steward on the Kalman Imre he never showed anyone to their compartment. Obviously he never attended the Romanian school of customer service. I presented him my ticket, and he pointed to a coach near the head of the train that looked like first class. I reviewed my ticket, which stated I was in 2nd class. So, I confirmed with him again and he asserted it was the correct carriage and I was in a two berth deluxe compartment.

My compartment was halfway up the car and on first review it looked no different to the compartment on the Kalman Imre until I opened a door and discovered it was en-suite. I presumed that was the deluxe part.

The Ister is a Romanian Sleeping car with 1, 2, and 3-berths with a wash-hand basin identical to the Kalman Imre. In addition, it had a couchette car with 6-berth and 4-berth compartments. I was in a deluxe compartment with my own private toilet and shower. The sleeping area was a lot wider than the one I had on the Kalman and it looked less like a Sailors bunk and more like a squaddies single bed. There was supposed to be a dining car, but I never bothered searching for it I was full up from the meal and had brought my own supplies along. Overall, I was happy with the Ister accommodation and the dread of being confined for sixteen hours soon left me.

Poor Liam had a ticket for a seat in the couchette car and it looked like he was sharing it with four other people. I felt sorry for him, and offered him the top bunk in my compartment, and I told him he would have to negotiate the upgrade with the steward. So, as we were about to get underway Liam approached the steward about the upgrade. However, the way he went about it looked as though he was trying to bribe him. The steward got a bit annoyed and turned him down and ordered him to get back to his own coach. I think if he had waited until everyone was on board and let the train take off then made a discrete approach the steward may have sorted him out. Later, he bribed another steward with 10 Euros and got a whole couchette to himself.

I got settled into my en-suite compartment and as it was

early evening and still light; I cleared out my backpack and repacked it to ensure it was ready for the next part of my trip. After I watched the Ister make its way into the Great Hungarian Plain (Nagy Alföld) I drifted off to sleep. I was feeling the effects of travelling; in the last 24 hours I had travelled 1449 kilometers, the equivalent of going from Land's End to John O'Groats and further. It was not something I was used to. Also, it had been a full day in Budapest, no wonder I was tired.

Gods knows how long I had been asleep when someone banging on my door woke me up. I had no idea what time it was, and it was pitch black in compartment. I jumped out of the bed stood up to turn on the light, and for the life of me I could not find the switch. So, I opened the door half-dressed and standing there before me was a woman with piercing blue eyes, blonde hair and from the limited light it looked as though she was wearing sparkling diamond earrings. I thought am I dreaming has Tatiana Romanova arrived. Sadly not the blonde hair had a hat on with 'Police' written on it and she demanded to see my passport. Half asleep I mumbled 'please give me a moment' and looked for the document in my day sack. On holding it up she snatched it out of my hand and scanned it with a hand-held scanner, and for some unknown reason it was not going through. As I waited I tried to engage in small talk, asking her where we were, but she was not in the mood for polite conversation. The passport was handed back, and with not so much as a goodnight or a thank you, then she moved on to the next compartment.

It was the first time since leaving the Gare du Nord that someone had checked my passport, which was surprising as I was expecting to show it going into Hungary never mind out of it.

I went back to bed and tried to forget about the interruption, yet it must have been only thirty minutes later when my compartment door was flung open. Not even a knock, this time it was the Romanian Police.

The Romanian was nowhere near as attractive as the Hungarian as it was a man. However, he found the light switch, which was handy then demanded to see my passport. I reached down to my daypack again to get it out of the pocket, and to my horror it was not there, 'oh shit where did I put it'. I was sure I put it back after the Hungarian check, but no I could not find it. After, searching for the thing, patting the bed, and mumbling 'I am sure I put it there', my mind went into over drive and thoughts of spending the night in a Romania Police cell flashed before my eyes. Then the Police officer tapped me on the shoulder and pointed to the wash-hand basin. I smiled and said; 'ah yes I forgot I put it there, thanks'. He gave it a glance looked at me, then handed it straight back and said; 'welcome to Romania goodnight'. I lay back down on the bed drew in some air then tried to get back to sleep.

Before I started this trip, I knew they would subject me to passport checks, and when you are sleeping in a compartment and you do not know precisely where you are it is hard to guess when it will take place. When it takes place it can be alarming.

I could not get back into the rhythm of sleep so I got up opened the window and looked at Google Maps to see where I was. The GPS position revealed that the Ister was somewhere in the Arad County of Romania. There was still a significant distance to reach before the train was anywhere near Bucharest. I just closed my eyes and thought about why I had taken this train.

A tickling sensation woke me up it seemed as if someone was dripping icy water on my face; it was gently gliding down the side of my face cheek down on to my neck. I opened my eyes and could see that it was still dark, and I felt as though I had been asleep for hours. I sat up, peered at the window, and saw that it was raining heavily outside. It was the thunderstorm as predicted by the long-range weather forecast, and the Ister was running straight in to it. As for the water on my face it was coming through the top of the window I had left open. The rainfall was coming in sideways.

I got up to close the window, and when I fully opened my eyes; I saw leaves all over the top bunk. It was as if a horticulturist had gone mad with a chain saw. The place was completely covered with foliage. Looks like the Romanians do not cut back the linesides of their railway tracks in the Sighisoara area because it was all over my compartment. Then only thing I could do was to pick up all the leaves and shove them back through the window. It must have taken me about twenty minutes to clean the place.

For certain, if anyone official had stepped into that compartment at that exact time it would have looked very odd. How would you interpret a grown man in his underwear pushing leaves out of a moving train at 5am in the morning?

There was no way I was getting back to sleep, not now after the exertions of having rid half a forest from my compartment. I was totally awake. Like a clock-watcher I checked Google again to see where I was. The map revealed that the nearest town was Sibiu. The Ister was now smack bang in the heart of Transylvania!

As there was not much else to do I just sat and gazed out the window. The weather looked gloomy and there was not much of view at all. However, as the Ister went further east towards the mountains the rain ended, the fog disappeared, and the Sun came out in all its glory. It was then I got my first glimpse of the Southern Carpathian Mountains in the distance and they looked marvellous. Now I had a clear view of rural Romania, with its charming little villages, green pastures and wildflower meadows. There were Farmers tending their herds and elderly women with headscarf's cycling down dirt tracks. It was literally as the ecologist Dr Andrew Jones called it 'the last truly medieval landscape in Europe'.

After the Ister moved off the plain it climbed upwards through a hardwood forest. As it hit the mountain, it slowed right down giving an excellent view of the thick forest and the odd isolated house and village. It was not long before it sped up again as it zigzagged its way back down towards the town of Brasov. A medieval walled city that was earlier part of a significant trade route linking western Europe with the Ottoman Empire.

Bran is situated near Brasov and many Dracula fans get off the train here to visit the Castle. Making Brasov one of the most visited cities in Romania. I got off to stretch my legs and have a vape and watch the train engineers change the old JB Engine over. Another, thing I noticed whenever the train stopped was two people would appear and tap the wheels. This was something I had never ever seen before and wondered if they were testing for cracks in the wheels. However, after Googling it I found out that the practice was common in 'Eastern Europe' and 'they tap wheels with a long-handled hammer and listen to the sound made to determine the integrity of the wheel; cracked wheels, like cracked bells, do not sound the same as their intact counterparts (they do not 'ring true')'.

I had no desire to visit or stay in Brasov, even though seeing the city and the castle would have been interesting, but stopping off would have put me back a day as the trains to Bucharest only run through that area once a day. Anyhow, I was never a big fan of the Dracula movies I had watched as a kid. Mainly the 1970s Hammer House of Horror movies, and that 1922 Nosferatu movie totally freaked me out.

About thirty minutes later the train moved off from Brasov and ascended up through the Bucegi National Park and down towards the Ploiesti Oil fields. I knew the history of the oilfields and the part it played producing oil for the Nazis during World War 2. The place was a major target for the Allied Air Forces during the war. Particularly during 'Operation Tidal Wave' in 1943 when the US Air Force heavily bombed it. Sadly, the operation turned out to be a very costly one, with the loss of 53 aircraft resulting in the deaths of 660 aircrew members. The Operation never halted the oil production. After, the war the Communist regime took it over and used the revenue to rebuild Romania.

As the Ister moved along the Prahova Valley, the train steward appeared at the door with a small breakfast and my ticket. The breakfast was not as good as the Kalman. Nonetheless, that and my snacks I had was enough food to see me through until I reached Bulgaria. Having the en-suite bathroom was an amenity not to be wasted. So, I thought I would use the shower and have a good scrub before facing the heat and sweat of another train journey. Undeniably, it was the smallest shower ever, yet I squeezed into it and managed to close the door. Then I turned the tap on. All I got was something that resembled the spit you get from a pissed off Camel when it throws up over you. I thought bloody marvellous; I wonder who classes this as second class? Fortunately, I carried wet wipes, and I finished my ablutions with them. It would have to do until I got to Bulgaria and find a more suitable bathing venue.

To say it was a relief when the train pulled into Bucharest is an understatement. The sixteen-hour train ride from Budapest is enough to test any travellers' constitution. While, I felt an achievement in making such a long journey it was unquestionably a pleasure to be getting off the Ister. Albeit, the trip was definitely worth the experience. After all, I had just travelled on the 23rd largest railway network in the world, which made going from London to Glasgow feel like a day trip!

As I hit the platform at Bucharest's Piața Gării de Nord

station, I spotted four men loitering at the platform exit. Two of them either side, it was like walking the gauntlet, and they looked as if they were hustling passengers as they went past. From, what I could make out they were asking if you needed a Taxi or if you fancied parting with your money. Either way, I stuck my head down and just ignored them. As I went past them they tried to grab my attention, but I kept focused and to their disappointment, looked right past them. I always find in situations like that its best never to make eye contact with them, just act as though they do not exist. It was the first time on my journey I came across hustlers, and it was something I was wary off and was looking out for the further I went east.

On the other side of the exit Liam was waiting for me, he was staying in Bucharest that night so it was the end of our journey together. We exchanged numbers and agreed to keep in touch throughout the trip which was a good thing as it was like a buddy-buddy system. We could check up on each other to see if all was ok and if it went belly up, then there was someone in the country who could help. I wished him good luck, and headed for platform 4, which was my embarkation point for Bulgaria.

6

VIDELE

InterCity Train 461 was packed. Probably because it is one of the few trains that goes direct from Bucharest to Sofia. Every day, it leaves at 12.45pm and arrives in Sofia about 22.28pm. Luckily, I had a reservation for coach 474, and another seat right by the window, which was a bonus as it was boiling. Seat 56 was in a Romanian six-berth 1970s/80s style couchette carriage. Comfortable enough if there are only two of you in it. However, not in mine there was an American from New York (Yankee), going all the way to Sofia, a New Zealander (Kiwi) travelling to the Black Sea resort of Varna and three German girls, likewise going to the resort.

The train was full of people all mainly going to Varna. It was known as the Red Riviera during the Communist period and was the holiday destination of choice for those prohibited from visiting the West. Specifically, the hierarchy of the erstwhile German Democratic Republic. Varna is now Bulgaria's third largest city, and it has firmly established itself as a holiday destination on a par with the likes of Benidorm in Spain.

After squeezing in to my seat I introduced myself to the Kiwi sat straight across from me. He was older than me and

looked like a seasoned traveller. I thought he was a long way
from home and what a lengthy way to come just for a cheap
holiday. Perhaps something else was drawing him there, I did
not bother enquiring? The Yankee never said much, except to
say where he was from and where he was going. He kept himself
to himself. The Germans just said, 'hello'. It was hardly the cast
from *Murder on the Orient Express*. Although, it was certainly
international.

Just as we all had settled some guy stuck his head into the
couchette looking solemn. He was well turned out in white
shirt, black trousers and had an official looking pass around his
neck. At first, I thought he was a train steward wanting to look at
our tickets. He spoke to us in Romanian, and then he broke into
German. I could not understand a word he was speaking.
However, I could see that the German girls were looking angst.
So, I presumed he was after money. After receiving no response
from the Germans, he suddenly spoke English, and fluent he
was too. It turned out he was a representative of a children's
charity and he was collecting donations. Almost in unison, the
American the Kiwi and me said, 'no thank you'. He then stared
straight at me and said, 'you must have some foreign currency', I
replied 'afraid not I gave it all to your friends on the platform'. The Romanian looked dejected, and quickly moved on.

The fact is, I do not mind giving to charity and I appreciate
there are children's homes in Romania that lack support, but
within fifteen minutes of being in a country and getting hustled
for cash I go straight on the defensive. However, I do not wish to
tar all Romanians with the same brush. I am certain I just
bumped into the kind of characters, who know the 12.45 to Sofia
is a good opportunity to get some extra Lev. I was glad I had
stuck to my initial plan to not stop in Bucharest.

As soon as the Romanian person had left another traveller
turned up at the door saying he had a reservation for a seat in

our compartment. However, all the seats were taken, and no one was leaving. The guy was not impressed, and he was not going. He called on the train steward to sort it out. I double-checked my ticket, and I was in the correct coach and in the proper seat, so I was not budging. It turned out one of the German lady's seat was in dispute and from the tone of the intense conversation she was not moving. From what I could tell between the lines of at least three different languages being spoken at the same time there had been a double booking, which baffled the steward. Not only that, the kerfuffle that ensued was delaying our departure. After considerable debate and the German lady blatantly refusing to surrender her seat all the steward could do was find the young man another seat in another carriage. The impasse was an eventful start to this part of the journey. Luckily, I would only be on the train for about three and a half hours.

I had planned not to go all the way to Sofia even though I was on a train heading there. I booked to go as far as Russe on the Bulgarian border where I would pick up the overnight connection to Sofia. If it all worked to plan, I would get in to the Bulgarian capital for about 6am.

The train pulled out of Bucharest and headed south west then south east across the Romanian Plain towards Videle a small town between Bucharest and Russe.

Videle is a major railway junction for trains going to Bulgaria. The place gained International notoriety after the collapse of socialism in Romania as a place with a hidden and sinister secret.

During the 1960s the childbirth rate decreased in Romania because of a laissez-faire approach towards abortion. The drop in the population had a direct impact on the economy. Therefore, the General Secretary of the Romanian Communist Party Nicolae Ceausescu and the Communist Party ratified the natalist 'Decree 770'. This totalitarian decree outlawed the practice of abortion and made birth control illegal for women under a certain age. To carry out the decree, Ceausescu banned the selling of contraceptives and placed his entire female population under state surveillance. The party even requested that woman receive monthly check-ups by gynaecologists. All women discovered to be pregnant were closely monitored right up to conception. Ceausescu even assigned his Secret Police to monitor all medical procedures during childbirth. In addition, they changed the focus on Sex education to emphasise it was a citizens' patriotic duty to provide the motherland with children.

Under these stringent conditions, the only women allowed to have an abortion were those who had more than four kids already or were over 45 years of age or they conceived the baby because of rape or incest. The impact of the decree resulted in a baby boom, leaving thousands of families who could not afford to have children forced to have them. Sadly, this later led to thousands of babies being placed in state-run institutions. Most of them hidden away in the Carpathian Mountains, out of sight and out of mind from society. The rise in orphaned children meant that the state could not care for them, which led to their neglect. Many children became emaciated, illiterate, and incapable of communicating with their state carers.

Fortunately, as the wind of change spread across the Iron Curtain, they ousted the Ceausescu regime in December 1989. The despot and his wife Elena were tried and convicted in a hastily lead show trial, which culminated in them both being shot on Christmas Day 1989. Subsequently, it was not until early 1990 when European aid agencies studying the soaring rates of AIDS amongst Romanian children discovered approx. 15,000+ abandoned kids. The discovery exposed the dreadful legacy of a despotic Communist system to the outside world.

Videle was one such Town that contained what the Romanians called 'Home for the deficient and unsalvageable'. On describing the living conditions of the Videle home one French Doctor at the time stated it is 'something between Auschwitz and Kampuchea'. I for one recall the pictures on the TV News channels of these kids' homes extremely well. It was disturbing to learn at the time that such a system existed in the 20th Century.

No one got off at Videle, as there really is nothing of interest to see.

7

ACROSS BRIDGE 889

The train pushed off from Videle through the fields and forests of Teleorman County. I was now in South Romania the region known in English as 'Greater Wallachia', and in Romanian as 'Muntenia'. It has a rich historical past. I liked the 14th Century Hungarian name for it 'Havaselvew' meaning, 'Land beyond the snowy mountains'. It gives that impression that at some stage in the region's history no one knew what was behind the snowy mountains. However, the train had left the Mountains behind after coming out of the Prahova Valley. The scenery from Videle to the border crossing point of Giurgiu was flat farmland with some rolling hills.

Romania and Bulgaria are in the European Union and are part of the Schengen agreement. Still, they have not implemented it yet. So, the train halted at Giurgiu for the compulsory passport checks. As soon as the Police were finished checking everybody's credentials the train proceeded at a low speed. I checked Google to see what was in front. Then I realised the train was about to pass over the magnificent Danube. Also, a very important bridge.

The Danube provides a natural border between Romania

and Bulgaria. It comprises a few crossing points, and if you are crossing by train, you will (at the time of writing) cross it by going over the striking steel girded Truss Danube bridge formerly known as the 'Bridge of Friendship'. The demand to bridge the divide (excuse the pun) between western and central Europe with the Balkan Peninsula goes back to the Crimean War of the 1850s. However, according to the Bulgarian National Radio website it was not until after World War 2 that official negotiations took place to construct and erect a bridge. The Central Committee of the Communist Party approved the project for a bridge on the 11 March 1950; they gave it the secret project name '889'.

They believed the project so strategically and geopolitically important to the Eastern Bloc that the Soviets took control of the entire project and nominated their own Department of Road Communications to oversee its construction. The Russians appointed Leonid Saprikin as the site manager, and two Soviet Engineers V. G. Andreev and N.N Rudomazin were tasked to design a bridge then build it.

Construction of the bridge started in 1952 and completed in 1954, which is not bad going considering the bridge is just shy of 2.5 km. It further tells you something about the strategic importance the Russians placed on requiring a bridge built that quickly. Overall, its structure was an Eastern Bloc effort. Romania and Bulgaria provided the labour. They brought the building materials from all corners of the Bloc countries. Later on, in 1959 both Andreev and Rudomazin designed and erected the Luzhnetsky Metro Bridge in Moscow, which looked very similar to the Bridge of Friendship, however that bridge was built using pre-pressed concrete and never lasted as long as the Danube Bridge before that needed restoration. As you move across the bridge, the view of the Danube is superb.

Once I arrived at the Bulgarian border, I felt a sense of

accomplishment come over me, or perhaps it may have been relief on reaching terra firma after being suspended 98 feet above a wide fast-flowing river. Either way, I was happy that I reached Bulgaria it had only taken two-and-a-half days. I was now in south eastern Europe, and I was nearly at the halfway point in my journey.

The first stop on the Bulgarian border was Russe Central Station, and it was my time to get off. However, before anybody could leave the train the Bulgarian Police arrived on board, took our passports off us, and vanished into the station. It was odd; as they do not explain to you what they are doing or how long they will be. I did not know whether to get off and follow them or just stay on the train. After thinking about it I got off and followed the officers into the station. However, with them being Government officials they had a right of way across the railway tracks, where I had to use the subway. So, I lost them going in to the station.

Russe station was large inside and sparse looking. All the signs, well the odd one that was there, was in Cyrillic not something I understood. I wandered around the ground level and could see nothing resembling a Police office. On hearing voices above me I glanced up and spotted two Policemen leaning over a balcony smoking. I headed upstairs towards them and after walking past several old empty rooms I located the Police station. Inside were two Policewomen scanning and scrutinising all the Passports. I tapped on the door and said, 'pardon me' to get their attention, and they ignored me. I knocked louder, and again the just blanked me. After standing at the door for about ten minutes I looked at the Policemen standing at the balcony smoking, they just smirked at me then looked away. So, I took a seat in the corridor and sat it out until the Policewoman had finished.

About twenty-five minutes had passed when the female

Sergeant came out with a bunch of various coloured Passports. Like a well-coiled spring I jumped off the seat and waved
at her. I must have looked like a lunatic, yet it was enough to
make her stop. She spun around and with a stern look on her
face gave me what sounded like a tirade of abuse in Bulgarian. I
never understood a word and for all I know she might have
simply said, 'wait your turn'. I just smiled at her and tried to
explain the best I could that I was stopping in Russe and was not
continuing to Sofia. She looked bewildered because she could
not understand me either. So, I just pointed to the Passports then the penny dropped. She worked through them took
one out studied my face then handed it over with an enormous
smile. I exhaled with relief then thought welcome to Bulgaria
Kevin.

Russe or 'Little Vienna' as they call is Bulgaria's fifth largest
city. It sits on the right side of the Danube and is noted for its
19th Century architecture. As I had about seven hours to kill
before my next train, I thought it would be a good place to see. I
expected I would just drop my backpack at left luggage and
spend the time exploring it. I went around the interior of the
station again, and I could not locate the international symbol for
left luggage, which is a 'Suit Case with a Key'. As I explained
previously there was a severe shortage of signs, in fact the
station was far from tourist friendly. They had an information
desk, so I went to that. I asked the woman perched behind the
counter 'govorish li angliïsk' she replied no and then ushered
me to the ticket counter. So, I approached the next woman sat
behind the ticket counter and asked her if she spoke angliïsk.
She grinned and replied, 'I speak a little', I responded with 'ah
good is there a left luggage area' she grinned again and shook
her head, which I was about to take as a yes then she said, 'no'.

Russe station is like the Clapham Junction of Bulgaria. Trains from all over the country pass through the place so I

was amazed that there was nowhere to leave my back-pack. With my expectations dashed and nowhere to leave my backpack safely I was left with two options, carry it around Russe City Centre for seven hours or hang around an empty station for seven hours. I did not fancy either option.

I went back up the stairs to the station platform searching for a café or some place I could rest and think of my next move. On going up and down the platform there was no café's, not even a shop. It was becoming clear that there was a severe lack of facilities at the station, which was very disappointing given its size. The interior of the station was rather nice, everything was marble, the floors, the walls, and there were these two massive, beautiful stone type chandeliers hanging from the ceiling in the main hall it looked like and important station at one stage in its life. Now it was just a shell!

In the main hall there was an information board where it showed the history of the station and the Bulgarian State Rail-ways (BDZ), specifically the Russe-Varna line. It turns out the Scottish Barclay Brothers with investment from William Glad-stone, built the line in 1864. This led to the need for a station at Russe. With the building of the Friendship Bridge BDZ built a new 'Grand Central Railway Station', in 1955 the very one I was standing in. However, like most Eastern Bloc Government buildings built in the 1950s they were designed in the Stalinist Empire style. So, everything was big. Moreover, you could see that there had been an attempt to modernise the place with the addition of two elevators. However, both were out of order and looked like they had been for years.

After exploring the inside, I headed out of the Station via two colossal wooden doors on to Aleksandŭr Stamboliys-ki Square named after a former Bulgarian President. As soon as I stepped outside the heat and humidity hit me, it was late after-noon, and it was sweltering. Now I knew why the station was

built with a marble interior. Going outside reminded me of the
old western Cowboy movies when the stranger emerges from
the station and tumbleweeds roll by, and the dust rises. Well, it
was almost like that, and for a minute or two it looked like a one-
horse town. The outside of the station looked nothing like the
inside, it looked dilapidated. Although, the facade looked as
though it was a grand station at one time it was now shabby and
exhausted looking. I thought to myself Stalin would turn in his
grave if he saw the state of his architecture now, its days of
grandeur had left many years ago, probably at the same time as
Communism.

I sat under the shade of a tree and chastised myself for not
doing a more thorough job on researching the station and its
facilities. Again, I toyed with whether to hang around a
deserted station all day and give up the opportunity of seeing
Little Vienna or lug a backpack around in the soaring heat. I
carried out a search on Google to see what facilities where
nearby and to my surprise it showed that there was a Metro
station nearby. I thought great I can get the underground to
Russe City Centre and take it from there. The location of the
Metro station was showing as being just a few hundred meters
away to the right of the central station. So, I got up put on my
backpack and headed towards it.

As I got near the station, I could see many people coming
and going with bags so I thought there must be shops and cafés
there too, hence why they are not in the station. It lifted my
spirits with the thought of getting a refreshing drink then
heading down town via the underground system. There was no
need to hang around the station after-all.

I walked up the stairs towards the station concourse and
there were people getting in and out of mini-buses, and many
people standing about with suitcases and bags it looked busy. I
looked around for the entrance to the underground, but I could

not see one, not even an escalator. Slightly confused with the layout of the station I asked a mini-bus driver if he spoke English and he said, 'yes' so I asked him where the underground was; he laughed and said, 'there was not one in Russe'. It turns out the Metro station is the mini-bus station and not an underground Metro station.

Feeling rather dispirited I found a bench and just sat there for about an hour in a daze watching the locals getting on buses going all over Bulgaria, places like Plovdiv, Burgas and Pleven. By this stage the heat had reached about 25 degrees and I was desperately in need of some refreshment, and the café's in the mini-bus station were more like Kebab shops and they did not look appealing. Therefore, I got up to look for something else more convivial to my likening.

I walked out of the station on to the Boulevard Tsar Osvoboditel and looked around. My eyes caught the corner of a building that looked like a shop next to a housing estate about 250 yards away. I went to have a look, as there was nothing to lose and everything to gain at this stage. As I got closer my eyes were right, it was a bakery, and it was closed. But now I was on Borisova Ulica and that had plenty of shops on it including one called 'Donald Duck', which made me chuckle.

On walking down Borisova in the direction of Russe City Centre I spotted sun canopies in the distance outside what looked like a block of flats. They were the same canopies you normally see in an English beer garden, and as I got closer, I saw they had *Stella Artois* written on them. I could hear Handel's Messiah singing in my brain 'Hallelujah' it is a pub. As I got even closer, it turned out to be a local hotel come restaurant called Kocmoc (Cosmos).

A sense of joy came over me as the place looked like a safe and good place I could easily sit for a few good hours. I went straight into the reception and tried my Bulgarian again. A man who I believe was the Manager nodded from side to side, and I remembered that in Bulgaria nodding up is 'no' and side to side is 'yes'. Therefore, he indicated that he spoke English. I asked him if it was ok to sit outside on the terrace and order food and drinks, the reply came back 'please be my guest' then he showed me to a table and said he would send someone out with an English menu for me. I felt elated and thought I can easily stretch this out for a good few hours.

When I was doing my research on the customs and traditional differences of each country I was going through, I came across the story behind the etiquette of the Bulgarian reverse head nodding. Apparently, it goes back to when the Ottoman army captured Orthodox Slavic Bulgarians. The Ottoman's being Muslim would try to force the Slavs to convert to Islam, and the method of persuasion was to hold a sword to their throat. The Bulgarians being true to their Slavic faith would just commit suicide by shaking their heads up and down against the sword blade. Therefore, they would rather kill themselves than submit to Islam. So, legend has it the nodding up and down became a gesture of defiance.

A young Bulgarian waitress came out of the Kocmoc and headed straight over to me. She said she spoke a little English and she would take my order. From the menu I ordered a Chicken dish, which she explained tasted like a Kebab with a Shopska salad. I also ordered the local Kamenitza lager. The Kebab came out in a clay pot and was more like a stew with veg, slightly spicy, and full of flavour it was just great staple food, which I was in need of. The lager was very cold and refreshing. On looking at the bottle contents it was only 2% alcohol, and it had lemon and grapefruit in it, no wonder it was so refreshing.

After I washed down the meal with the Kamenitza, I ordered another lager, and asked for one a little stronger. The young waitress advised me that the normal lager was strong. I told her I was Scottish and before I could say anything more; she giggled nodded the European way and trotted off to get one. She had heard of the Scots reputation with alcohol then. So, I polished another lager off and then another, and I completed the meal with a Turkish coffee. The waitress told me they make the best one in Russe, and I can safely vouch for that claim it was indeed excellent.

By the time I was finished at the Kocmoc five hours had flown by and it was time to walk back up Borisova Ulica to Stalin's Grand Railway station. Deep down inside I was disappointed that I never explored Russe. However, at least I have seen the local side of the place and sampled real Bulgarian hospitality. I was thoroughly refreshed and ready for the next part of my journey to Sofia.

I asked, for the bill, and the cost for one meal, three beers and one coffee came to the equivalent of six pounds, which was exceedingly cheap compared to London, well compared to anywhere really. With the price being so low I left a reasonable tip as I felt it was only right, they had had been very hospitable, and I had felt safe and welcome in their restaurant. On leaving, I made a point of popping inside and said farewell to the Manager and the waitress and left a happy customer. It is this type of hospitality that warms you to different cultures. I vowed to myself if I ever go back through Russe I would definitely visit the Kocmoc again.

Apart from a Policeman, smoking a big fat cigar on platform 1 was totally deserted. The night train to Sofia was scheduled to arrive at 10.55pm. As it got closer to the time, it looked like it would be a very lonely night. Then I spotted two guys eyeing me up from across platform 2. Not before long they walked across the tracks and were on my side of the platform. In that part of the world, it is not unusual to see people walk across train tracks rather than use the underpass. I even saw stray dogs cross what looked like electric tracks then go under trains and appear on the platform, it is not something you see at English railway stations, definitely not in central London. The two guys took up a seat just a metre or two away from me and they looked different to the locals I had seen at the Kocmoc. They looked more like drifters, and my instincts were telling me they were trouble.

Before I went on the trip, I did some research about travelling in the wee hours of the morning, especially in remote areas. I found an article about train robberies and even sexual assaults specifically on the night trains between Romania and Bulgaria. So, I knew that a potential threat existed. Analysing that threat I thought I am unlikely to be sexually assaulted, but there is a definite possibility of being robbed. Anyway, I kept these two suspects in sight, and I made sure they knew I was aware of them.

It was about 10.50pm and I could see the BDZ train lights about two kilometers away in the distance, then suddenly from nowhere a crowd of teenagers appeared on the platform, then three Policemen came out of a doorway and stood on the platform, then more people turned up. In a matter of minutes, the station was busy, and it looked like it would not be a lonely night after-all. As I stated at the beginning of the book, it is not unusual for people to turn up at the last minute for a train and Russe was a prime example.

Bridage 889, 1955, courtesy of Bulgarian National Radio

Russe Central Station, Bulgaria

8

EMERGENCY AT PAVLIKENI

The regional night train to Sofia pulled up at exactly 10.55pm. I had no reservation for this train as they advised me that there would be plenty of seats, and there was a possibility I would get a whole compartment to myself.

Halfway up the train I found an empty carriage two cars down from the two dodgy looking guys. I had a whole couchette to myself and was looking forward to a peaceful night and sprawling out on one of the seats.

The peacefulness was shattered when all the teenagers moved into the couchette next door and descended into full party mode. Then, a Mother and her daughter joined me, so that put an end to having it to myself. Actually, I did not mind that at all; it felt safer to share with them and I wondered if they joined me for that same reason. Also, I noticed that the three Policemen I saw standing on the platform got on board and took up seats on either side of the train, and one was situated in the middle. I sort of wondered if there had previously been trouble on this train in the past?

Shortly just after 11pm the train got under way and headed

south through the Veliko Tarnovo Province of north central
Bulgaria. This Bulgarian province is very rural. It is known as
the medieval capital of Bulgaria and it is another area of significant historical importance. Apparently, on this route the train
goes through some of the most scenic parts of the country. Pity I
was going through it during the night, as I am sure the view
would have been interesting.

After about three hours at a steady speed, the train stopped
at Gorna Oryahovitsa for the obligatory swapping over of
Engines and the ritual of wheel tapping. Everyone in my
carriage got off the train for a smoke and the teenagers disappeared to the shop on the far platform, no doubt to stock up on
alcohol. I got off to stretch my legs and have a vape and see
where the two drifters were, and I could not see them.

So far, I was enjoying the ride and I remember thinking to
myself in four hour's time I will be in Sofia, and I will have a nice
big breakfast, and not to forget to sort out your reservation for
Belgrade! I was happy I had met all my trains, and everything
was going as I planned it!

With nothing else to do at Gorna I went back to the
couchette and got my head down. I wished that I had brought a
lightweight sleeping bag, it would have come in really handy at
this point. After settling down I put my headphones on,
pumped up the volume to drown out the chugging sound of the
train and the teenage party next door. Not before long I fell
asleep listening to U2's Zooropa album.

I must have been dozing for about an hour when my nostrils
detected the hint of smoke. It was not like the smell you get from
burning wood, it was more like the smell of an electrical fire, it
was noxious. I shrugged it off as with these old 1970s – 80s trains
you get the odd whiff of burning rubber. So, I was not bothered
about it I had become accustomed to it.

Again, I drifted off to the sound of Bono, then suddenly I was vigorously shaken. I opened my eyes to see it was the Mother, who was sharing my compartment, and she was shouting something at me. Then I saw her daughter crying and looking distraught. I whisked off my headphones and shot up to see what was going on, but it was dark. There was no light on in the couchette; the only light coming in was from the passageway. At first, I could not see anything unusual, yet the smell of smoke was strong. No fire or smoke alarms were going off. So, I opened the compartment door and discovered that the passageway was filling up with smoke. It was so heavy it looked as if someone was pumping it into the train, it was filling up fast.

Reluctantly I stuck my head out of the window which is not generally a good idea because of the lack of trimming on the linesides. However, I needed to know if the train was on fire! All I could see was a thick cloud of smoke billowing out from underneath our carriage. By this stage, the young daughter and Mother were frantic with worry. Then a train steward came running down the passageway looking pretty anxious. Again, I looked out of the window searching for the glimmer of a fire. However, I saw nothing, just thick smoke; it did not look good. I tried to calm the daughter and her Mother down, but the language barrier got in the way. Then my Army training kicked in. I kept thinking remain calm and look for a way to escape.

Our carriage was now rapidly filling up with smoke so much, so I had to put my handkerchief, the one I carried around with me to soak up the sweat with, over my mouth and nose. I then ushered the young woman and her Mother to another carriage further up the train. Then I felt the train coming to an emergency halt. You could hear the brakes hissing and screeching as it was breaking, it was a relief.

I did not fancy jumping off a moving train into the Bulgarian wilderness at 3am in the morning. However, I was prepared to do just that if it did not stop. The train stopped at Pavlikeni station. Waiting on the platform were two Police officers and two BDZ engineers, yet there was no fire engine? I looked at Google Maps to see how far we were from a major city, but I could not get a signal. Given the time I guessed we must have been just north of the Balkan National Park. Basically, we were in the middle of nowhere.

Everyone got off the train and assembled on the platform, and some passengers even took off altogether and headed for the exit. Then the engineers went underneath the train with torches looking for the source of the smoke. I saw no one with a fire extinguisher so guessed there was not a fire and some Policemen were laughing, which looked odd. I supposed if they did not think it was worth evacuating everyone then it cannot be that serious.

Not long after the engineers went under the train, they popped their heads up from underneath and started yelling at the train driver, then started banging away at something right under my carriage. There continued a lot of yelling and a lot of banging, yet no one seemed in panic.

I stood there on the platform watching the BDZ staff shouting at each other and the Police laughing thinking what a joke. Then I started to wonder what I would do if they took the train out of commission. I had no Bulgarian Lev, although I had Euros and US Dollars and both currencies would get me anywhere, I needed to go. Nonetheless, I was a long way from Sofia, and it was the 'Devils hour' 3am. The only other option I could think of was to stop at the station until dawn and get another connection.

The banging and yelling went on for about thirty minutes. Suddenly this guy appeared from the station and started screaming at the train driver, who was most noticeable because he had a significant limp. He was the third train driver I had spotted on my trip who had a limp, and wondered if it had anything to do with industrial accidents?

The individual doing the shouting and screaming looked official. I suspected he must have been the stationmaster. Whoever he was the BDZ staff and Policeman stood to attention every time he barked an order. As soon as he stopped shouting the Police ushered everyone back on board. Though not everyone was prepared to chance it. A lot of people headed for the exit again. I was dithering whether to stay or go. I reconsidered my options and decided to risk it. I thought to myself just stay vigilant and be prepared to jump off the train if it happens again.

I re-boarded the Bulgarian trailblazer and grabbed my backpack and moved along with everybody else to a carriage right at the rear of the train. At least I was near the backdoor if I needed to escape.

As I sat down It dawned on me why the bus station at Russe was much busier than the train station, probably because no one trusts the trains.

I had never factored in train safety or fires when I was planning the trip. Train disasters are such a rare thing in the UK that the chances of being caught in one never passed over my mind. In all my research going through online blogs, and YouTube videos I saw nothing reported, and there was nothing on Seat 61. However, as soon as I got a signal on my phone, I Googled it. My research threw up a few sobering stories. In 2008 the BDZ night train from Sofia to Kardam went on fire burning nine passengers alive and in 2009 a BDZ locomotive the same type that was pulling my carriage went on fire on its way from Pleven to Varna luckily no one was killed. From the number of online articles, it suggested train fires were commonplace in Bulgaria!

This leads to the story of train travel in Bulgaria, which is interesting. During the Communist era, most Bulgarians never owned a car so going by train was the primary mode of transport. BDZ was the favoured company of the party. To have a position with BDZ was for the privileged elite. The staff got lots of benefits, a decent wage, and indeed a bonus. However, it all went from good too bad after the collapse of socialism in 1989. Capitalism allowed Bulgarians to buy cars, which led to fewer people travelling by train. So, financially BDZ struggled to maintain the trains and pay its work force. From what I read It was no surprise that the trains were somewhat risky!

As we went further, south towards Pleven I was fighting a battle to remain awake. I was continually bungee necking. If you have ever been on a hard stag in the Army you will know what that feels like. If you have not, it feels like your neck is one big elastic band and you cannot keep your head up, it just bounces back down again. At that stage I had been on the move for about 18 hours. Anyway, sleep won, and I dozed off.

I had only been asleep for a few minutes when I felt someone or something touch my arm, whatever it was it caused me to jump up. As I opened my eyes and looked around the old woman sat across from me was glaring at me and uttering something alien. I thought perhaps I was snoring, and it was irritating her, plus I talk in my sleep so maybe I was keeping her awake. Anyway, when I looked at the time, I had not been a sleep for a few minutes I had been sleeping for over two hours. Whoever or whatever caused me to wake up I was glad they or it did as the Sun was coming up and the view was looking good. I checked my phone and there was a full signal and Google was showing my position was near Svoge, which lies in between the Iskar Gorge and the Iskar River.

The train had made up good time since the emergency stop and it was now descending towards Novi Iskar in the Sofia

Valley. I felt relieved that I was now not that far away from the Bulgarian Capital.

This train journey was one adventure I will not forget in a long time and perhaps one I would not suggest doing overnight. I would much prefer to do it during the day so I can look at the magnificent scenery, specially the Iskar Gorge.

As the Russe train drew into sunny Sofia at 6.30am, I had another feeling of accomplishment; I had made it to the halfway point. The hard part of my journey was over. The remaining train journeys would be a breeze.

9

GLADSTONE STREET

S ofia can trace its history back some 7000 years. So, it is one of the oldest cities in Europe if not the world. Sadly, it has not yet made it into the top 10 cities of the world list. However, it was a place I wanted to see.

On Rail Europe's website for Sofia they state it is the place for the 'wonderer and wanderer' to have coffee and tell whoever will listen about how long you took to get there. Well, whoever was prepared to listen I would tell them it took me just over three days to get there from London. Anyhow, when I got off at the Central train station all I wanted was a coffee and a breakfast. I was in no mood to discuss the events of the last 72 hours.

The Central station is modern compared to Budapest's Keleti pályaudvar and Bucharest's Piaţa Gării de Nord. Also, it was very vibrant for 7am on a Saturday morning.

I went in search of a café and after wandering around the station I found this little bakery in the under ground area; you could literally smell the freshly baked pastries coming from the place. It looked ideal for what I was looking for, somewhere quiet and tucked away.

The main offering on sale was the local breakfast dish of

'Banitsa', which is Feta cheese wrapped in filo pastry. It looked good, and a bit heavy looking for breakfast. I thought well when in Rome! So, I asked the old woman behind the counter if she spoke English and she waved her hand to indicate a little, which was good enough for me. I pointed at the Banitsa and then the coffee machine showing the hand signal for a large one. The old woman had a very nice welcoming smile and looked as though she enjoyed receiving tourists. She said, 'Ciao' to everyone when they left, which I thought was very cosmopolitan. However, it is quite common to hear the words Ciao and even Merci being spoke in Sofia.

After taking my order, she welcomed me to take a seat and served up the warm local dish with a coffee that would wake you from a coma. I cared not, I was tired and hungry and would have settled for much worse. The pastry was soft and delicious, yet there was not much taste coming from the Feta cheese. But it was definitely edible and filling. The caffeine from the super strong coffee kicked in and brought me back to life. I was now able to focus on my plans for the day ahead.

For the journey to Serbia, I had two options book a seat or just chance it. The Sofia to Belgrade train apparently was never busy. Nonetheless, it was high season and sod's law states that if I did not reserve a seat, I would probably end up standing for nine hours or end up in with the sheep. When I first started reserving trains online it taught me not to believe everything I read. So, I paid the old woman for my coffee and Banitsa said, 'Ciao' and headed upstairs to the main concourse in search of the ticket counter.

In my best Bulgarian I asked 'Dobro utro govorish li angliĭsk' and the young lady behind the ticket desk replied 'a little', I asked her, 'do I need a reservation for the Belgrade train leaving tomorrow at 9.40am'. She told me I was at the wrong desk and needed to go to the International desk. The desk was virtually two steps to the right, but it was not open until 8am. With half an hour to wait, I went outside for a vape and some fresh air. When I got my vape out and started puffing away I instantly got some very funny looks, especially from members of the older generation. Then it occurred to me that I had hardly seen anyone vape all the way from Budapest to Russe. Vaping has not really taken off in central Europe as cigarettes are still popular, everyone smokes like a trooper.

It was just after 8am when the young woman decided to open the International desk. She looked pretty smart in her railway uniform. I asked her if she spoke English she nodded and replied 'yes'. So, I asked her about the Sofia to Belgrade train and was a reservation necessary; she sighed, rolled her eyes and said, 'it was'. I thought the sigh was strange and unnecessary. Perhaps, she gets asked that question a lot and is bored hearing it over and over again. Anyhow, I asked her for a window seat and paid her the equivalent of 1.25 Euros. Then she gave me a ticket for seat 56. I thought hold on that's twice I have had that seat number, the last time was from Bucharest to Russe, hey it could be my lucky seat number?

By the time I was finished with Sofia train station, it was about 9am. I was not expected at the Hotel Bristol until 2pm. So, I thought I would chance my arm and see if I could get in early. I was even prepared to pay extra for it.

On looking on the Hotel website for instructions on how to get there it seemed rather straightforward. According to the map the Hotel was right behind the Ramada Hotel, which was sticking out like a sore thumb on the skyline about one kilometre away. I decided that I would walk rather than get a taxi I had plenty of time to get there.

After walking for about a kilometre down the Knyaginya Maria Louisa Boulevard the Hotel was nowhere in sight. I checked the map again, and it looked like it was about another kilometre straight on. I got to the Lion's Bridge and walked across the Vladaya River and up a hill. I was not lost, yet the Hotel seemed a lot further away than the instructions given on the website. I walked another kilometre then turned right onto Tsar Simon Utica and 500 meters ahead I found Hristo Botev Boulevard and my hotel. On asking the receptionist about the route given on the website she pointed out I had followed the directions for driving. I had taken the one way road way route. She said if I had taken the direct walking route I would have been there in under twenty minutes. I made a mental note to read the instructions more carefully.

On checking in at the Bristol, I explained to the receptionist I had been travelling all night, and told her the story about the train nearly catching fire. I played on how little sleep I had, then I asked if could I get into my room early. The receptionist who spoke immaculate English and seemed very amiable looked straight at me and with a commanding voice said, 'sorry no check-in before 2pm'. I was disappointed to say the least, however rules are rules. Moreover, I never considered that the room might still be occupied after-all it was only 10.30am. So, I asked her if I could freshen up somewhere and leave my back-pack in the luggage area. Her response was far better than the first and she said, 'no problem' and showed me to the luggage room and guest bathroom.

After freshening up I left my pack secured in the room and took a seat outside on the terrace. I thought I would sit and rest for a while then look for a shop that sold vaping gear. It was a glorious morning. I could feel it was going to be another hot day, and it never felt as humid as Russe did. Moreover, It looked like a good day for a game of Golf based on the dress code of the Chinese men who came out of the Bristol. No doubt buisness men going off for a corporate game of gāo ěr fū.

According to Google, there were only two shops in Sofia that sold vaping juice, and one of them was on William Gladstone Utica (Street). Gladstone is a Bulgarian national hero. So, I was not surprised to find a street named after him. Besides investing in their railway system, he supported the Bulgarians and their bid for freedom from Ottoman rule.

He became the darling of Bulgaria after April 1876, when Nationalist Bulgarian Revolutionaries staged a revolt against their Ottoman Rulers. The Turks had suppressed them socially and politically for years. The upshot is that the uprising failed and the Turkish forces massacred thousands of Bulgarians, specifically in the town of Batak. It was estimated that the Turkish army and the Bashi-bozuk (irregular Turkish soldiers) headed by Ahmet Aga murdered over 5,000 men, woman, and children. They even beheaded those who would not convert to Islam, hence the nodding custom I pointed out previously. News of the slaughter reached all over Europe. The former British Ambassador in Sofia Steven Williams wrote in 2009, that Gladstone was 'absolutely shocked by the massacre of thousands of Bulgarians in the aftermath of the 1876 April Uprising, he published a poignant, polemic brochure, The Bulgarian Horrors and the Question of the east. In the course of just one month, the pamphlet sold 200,000 copies. Gladstone urged other prominent figures such as Giuseppe Garibaldi to join the Bulgarian cause. The campaign that he opened led to all-European demands for reforms in the Ottoman Empire. They contributed to Bulgaria's re-emergence as an independent nation in 1878. Gladstone's activities won him a heroic aura, and his name became popular in Bulgaria'.

William Gladstone is firmly sewn into the fabric of Bulgaria's history they have not merely named streets after him they have named Schools and indeed made documentaries about him.

After sitting outside in the sunshine for about thirty minutes trying to find the street on the map, the Hotel receptionist came out and with a huge smile said, 'your room will be ready in twenty minutes if you wish to take it now'. I thought there is a god after-all or perhaps Gladstone has looked down on me. Either way I was delighted.

They gave me room 205, on the second floor and up in the lift I went. My double room was tucked away at the end of the corridor. So, no view of Hristo Botev Boulevard then. Not that I was bothered I was planning on doing some laundry and hanging it out of the window to dry. It would not have been appropriate to hang it out from a facade facing window.

As soon as I opened the door to the room, I dumped every-thing on the bed, stripped off, and headed straight into the shower. As I turned the tap on I was praying please do not let it be a drizzle, I want blasted, and voilà the water came out at a rapid rate of knots.

Back when I was planning the trip I realised taking a daily shower between locations might be problematic. Nonetheless, I thought I would work that out along the way. Since the bath at Kiraly and this shower it seemed too long. Besides from now on in I was in a hotel every night so it would no longer be an issue.

A shower and change of clothes is as good as a rest in my books. So, with my morale fully restored, I set about getting some vital admin done. I emptied my backpack and repacked it; I put all batteries on charge, stuck my passport and valuables in the safe, and set the code number to 1642. A year engrained in my brain until the day I die. It was the year they formed the Scots Guards and kind of hard number to forget!

I gathered my set of travelling clothes hand washed them and hung them out the back window, which looked on to an enclosed courtyard. It was getting so hot outside that they would be dry in no time. Of course I could have had them professionally laundered, but it was just as easy to do it myself.

I stared at the big comfortable looking double bed and

thought about climbing into it and taking a catnap, but time was precious. I was only here for a day and I wanted to make the most of it. So, I went back down to the reception and sat for a while studying a tourist map I picked up at reception. So far, I had relied on Google Maps and it had not failed me. Also, I tried another phone app that was recommended called City Mapper. However, the app developers had obviously only got as far as Paris as it stopped responding the minute I left the Gare de l'Est. Moreover, I bought a burner phone specifically for the trip and an international sim card. The burner phone was inexpensive and if it had been lost or stolen it would not have been a big deal. The Sim card company stated that you got favourable rates when used on the continent, yet it was costing a small fortune on data usage. So, I thought I would switch to conventional methods and use a paper city map to get around Sofia.

So, fresh as a daisy, I trotted off in search of William Gladstone Street. After about one kilometre I found the beginning of the street. The houses on the street were very old they resembled the French apartment blocks you see in the 7th arrondissement of Paris. Also, some were definitely Stalinist era. Besides I was looking for a newer looking building. The images I had seen of the shop looked as if it was in a Mall. The shop I was looking for was called 'VapeMan'. I almost walked past the place before I noticed it. It was not exactly a Mall in the American context it was more like a couple of shops built under the one roof. I went in to the shop and asked the guy behind the counter if he spoke Angliĭsk? Few people in Bulgaria speak English; especially in the countryside, and with Sofia being a capital city I expected to encounter more speakers, specifically from the younger generation.

The VapeMan's English was fluent, probably because he was from Greece. He told me he had moved to Sofia three years before and opened a small E-cigarette business hoping it would take off in the capital. We spent about an hour debating the highs and lows of vaping throughout Europe. He was optimistic about the chances of vaping taking off in Sofia. Cigarettes in Bulgaria are about 2.50 Euros; so I expect he will be waiting a long time for the vaping revolution to reach Bulgaria. However, I admired his enthusiasm and made his day by spending a decent amount of Lev on vaping paraphernalia.

Mission accomplished, I now had to get cigarettes for my partner in the UK, when I gave up smoking she had stuck with the Marlboros. As I came out of the VapeMan's shop, I swung right on to Gladstone Street and headed towards the famous Vitosha Boulevard the central shopping place in Sofia. On the way, I spotted a hunting shop so popped in to have a look. You do not see these types of shops anymore in the UK because of the rise in knife crime. The shop was like an armoury, and he had a splendid display of hunting rifles and semi-automatic rifles, including the infamous AK47 Kalashnikov. I thought given the security situation in the West it was just as well we do not have those types of shops anymore. On speaking to the owner, he explained that hunting is big business in Bulgaria a number people in the countryside own guns and hunt wild boar and red deer. I thought who goes hunting with an AK47?

Vitosha Boulevard is full of well-named high street fashion outlets, and café bars are in abundance. It is vibrant, and the atmosphere felt good. I strolled up and down the central part, bought a few gifts, and later had lunch in one of the café's with a nice view of Vitosha Mountain.

After sitting watching and tuning in to all the various nationalities going up and down this fine thoroughfare I headed down towards the start of the boulevard, if it is indeed the start, yet it is the place where all the prominent buildings are nested.

St Nedelya Church, built around the 10th century. Then there are the Presidential buildings. I admired the look of the

1950s communist designed Hotel Balkan. Sadly, they built it on top of a Roman Fortress. I popped in to the Balkan's lobby bar 'Pliska' for an apéritif and to scope the place out for a prospective future visit. It is another splendid looking place, finely decorated inside and now owned by the Sheraton chain of Hotels. I sat at the bar wishing I had booked the Balkan rather than the Best Western. However, I decided I would come back one day and stay for a few days. There was plenty more to look at and do in Sofia that I could not fit into in one day.

After, a refreshing pint of Bulgarian lager I wandered towards the rear of the Balkan to the oldest Church I have ever been in. The 4th Century Roman built Church of St George, lies in the heart of the Roman complex 'Serdika'. It was the icing on the cake and indeed looks like a cake, with it being a Rotunda. The history of the place is awesome; if you travel to Sofia, you must visit it.

The last site on my walkabout was the 'Largo', which is a set of three Stalinist Empire style buildings again all built in the 1950s. One is now the department store TZUM, and very similar to TsUM in Moscow's Petrovka Street. The building straight across from TZUM's is the Bulgarian President's office, and the middle one, the most imposing one was the headquarters of the Bulgarian Communist Party right up until 1990. The Largo is a commanding feature in Sofia and you cannot miss it. Moreover, it is a documented fact that the buildings are some of the finest examples of 1950s Socialist-era architecture in south east Europe. Also, the golden faced black eyed statue of St Sofia stands at the Largo, she was placed there in 2000 to replace a statue of Vladimir Ilyich Lenin that was removed in 1990.

So, after a full day in Sofia I wandered back to Hristo Botev Boulevard in search of some supper. Across the road from the Bristol, there is a Turkish restaurant, so I thought I would try it. I popped in and had a look at the menu, but there was no

English translation. I struggled to understand the Cyrillic words and ended up just pointing to a scrumptious looking spicy sausage with salad and rice. The meal turned out to be ok, nothing special, and the Turkish coffee that followed was pretty good. Although, not as good as the Kocmoc's in Russe. As I was drinking my coffee minding my business a chap on the table next to me asked if I enjoyed my meal, I could tell it was a bid to have a conversation with me, or maybe he was trying out his English. He explained I had a meal in the best Turkish restaurant in the whole of Sofia. I would not burst his bubble by saying you should try the Kocmoc in Russe they do a mean Chicken kebab; instead I told him the meal was pleasant and the Turkish coffee was good. He then quizzed me about where I had been and where I was going and what was the purpose of my trip, his curiosity made me feel uncomfortable. By the standard of his questions, I think I bumped into an off-duty Police officer, or perhaps that is how Bulgarians are. Either way I was not in the mood to discuss my trip. So, I made my excuses and bid him goodnight then crossed the road and disappeared into room 205.

Morpheus had been generous and sent me into a deep sleep and when I awoke at 6.30am, I felt great and full of energy. After another great shower, I left room 205 in search of breakfast. The online reviews for Hotel Bristol had many comments about the breakfast; everyone had rated it as one of the best in town so I was looking forward to trying it.

Vitosha Boulevard, Sofia

The Balkan, Sofia to Belgrade

10

HOTEL MOSCOW

The breakfast at the Hotel Bristol was excellent. There was a good selection of food available, including carrots peas and broccoli for whoever likes having a roast dinner at 7.30am on a Sunday morning. If you ever go to Bulgaria, I would highly recommend you try the Yoghurt. It is on a par with Greek Yoghurt if not better, pity it is not for sale in the UK.

After a fulfilling breakfast, I picked up my backpack and checked out of my room and asked the receptionist for the quickest route to the train station. The young woman at the front desk showed me on a map and assured me that that the Train station was a leisurely twenty minute's walk straight down the Boulevard. The route she showed me was definitely different from the one I had taken the morning before.

Now, I was all set and ready to move on to the next part of my journey. Before leaving the Bristol, I wished them well, and I promised the receptionist I would leave a favourable review on Booking.com. The hotels in that part of the world rely heavily on reviews and the Bristol was no exception, they admitted me early and the overall standard of the hotel was high.

As I stepped on to the boulevard, there was a cool breeze coming down from Vitosha Mountain, yet I could feel it was going to be another hot day.

To get to the train station all I had to do was turn left and head directly south along Hristo Botev Boulevard named after a Bulgarian Poet and a National Revolutionary Hero. He died during the uprising of 1876 and was considered a symbol of anarchism and a patron of the sociological ideology, which the Bulgarian Communist Party played on for years.

The Bristol receptionist was right it did not take me long to reach Sofia Central station. The route was almost parallel to the one I had taken the day before, although it was at least a kilometer shorter. By the time I got to the station, it was about 18 degrees and getting hotter. On checking the weather forecast they expected it to reach about 22 degrees, by mid-day so I needed to find somewhere I could stock up with bottled water and snacks as the next part of my journey would be nine hours long.

Sofia Central Train Station is not as straightforward to navigate as it looks. It is a modern and spotless station compared to other Bulgarian stations. However, its 'Brutalist' style can deceive you into going in the opposite direction. Built in 1888 in the Baroque style it was demolished in 1971 and reconstructed by Milko Bechev in 1974. In my opinion it is very poorly designed, and I did not find it tourist friendly. For example, on the departure board all the place names are in Cyrillic, fortuitous for me I recognised the spelling for Belgrade. There are no signs pointing to the platforms in English and to locate them you have to go down to an underground level that is inadequately lit, and drab looking and if you do not know where you are going it can take you around in a circle until you locate the correct platform.

According to the departure board the next train to Belgrade

was leaving from platform 4. So, I set off right away to find it. I recalled the way I had arrived from the Russe train, so I headed the same way and not before long I spotted the entrance to the platform. On reaching the top of the stairs I noticed two graffiti covered rolling stock one Bulgarian, and the other was Serbian sitting on the rails. On closer inspection, I noticed a piece of paper taped to the window stating it was 'Carriage 463', which confirmed it was my train.

My heart sank as I thought the train would have been a lot more modern and a lot longer than just two carriages. By the condition of the carriages, it was evident that Belgrade was not a popular destination. I took a long hard look at the carriages and wondered if they would make it to Belgrade, either way, it was going to be an interesting trip. The condition of the carriages on the outside was awful, all the windows were all steamed up preventing anybody from peering inside. From top to bottom and side to side, they were both covered in graffiti, which was far from artistic. It was not even a couchette style carriage it was an open one.

Now I found the platform and my train known as the 'Balkan' I had one hour left to kill. Rather than go back upstairs to the central concourse I spent it in the little bakery I first went into the morning before. As I went in the elderly lady from yesterday was serving again and she gave me a friendly grin. I ordered one of her heavily caffeinated coffees and sat down to review all my documentation and work out what I would do once I got to Belgrade.

As the time drew nearer to 9.20am, I bought another coffee to take-away so I could get rid of off the Bulgarian Lev I had left over. I never had much left, and I did not wish to take it with me as it is not a popular currency in Serbia and the exchange rate was weak. The elderly woman brought me my coffee smiled and said 'Ciao', I retorted with the same convivial 'Ciao' and dumped the remaining Lev into her tip plate, she looked very surprised. No doubt it was a big tip just for two coffees, I hope I made her day?

I headed back to platform 4 and BDZ Engine 1490 was just being loaded on to the graffiti covered carriages. I climbed on board and searched for seat 56. However, sods' law there was an old couple sat in my seat no doubt because it was one of the few seats with clean windows on the whole carriage. Dam I thought if only I had been a little earlier, I would have got my seat. I never had the heart to ask the old folks to move, so I looked around for another one.

There were enough spare seats around, but you could barely see out of the windows. Nevertheless, I managed to find one with a reasonable view. I only hoped that no one else had booked the seat, as the train was starting to fill up. I sat there just staring out of the window praying the thing would take off. Luckily, few more people got on board and the Balkan roared up and took off. I stuck my headphones on and played the Beatles *Magical Mystery tour*, it seemed an appropriate tune to start the journey with.

The passengers on the Balkan were mainly backpackers; like me who were probably Interrailling it. I had picked up German and French accents on boarding then I heard the recognisable tone of English voices coming from a young couple that had arrived on board at the last minute. They were seated just up from me, and across from two French girls. It looked like it would be a peaceful trip, which pleased me, as I aimed to break up the trip by finishing my journal for Sofia, read my book, and then for the rest of the day I would lay back and feast my eyes on the Serbian countryside.

As we got further out of Sofia, I noticed the young English guy going up and down to the back door of the train. I suspected that he was going for a smoke and I was dying for a vape, so I kept my eye on him to see what he was doing. The thing is with some trains in the Balkans smoking is not rigorously enforced on them, so getting away with a cheeky cigarette out the back door was easy enough, you just did not make it obvious. I watched the young guy get up and head towards the back of the train again and I saw the outline of a cigarette pack in his trousers. I got up and followed him then asked him 'are you going for a cheeky cigarette', he smiled and said, 'yep I am' I said, 'me too'. So, I followed him to the back door of the train and found that the side door was wide open, and the back window was open, and it looked on to nothing, except for tracks. With one eye on the corridor watching for a guard and the other on the side door, we puffed and chatted away.

After a brief introduction the young man turned out to be Isaac who was travelling with his girlfriend Summer on a month-long trip through Europe. They had flown into Sofia the day before and spent the day exploring the sights, and from what they told me about their first day, they had seen more of Sofia than I had, but I was at my halfway point and on a schedule.

The train was running at a constant pace through Slivnitsa, heading northwest towards the Serbian border. The terrain looked beautiful, yet a lot of it was forested, and mountainous, with the odd rural village spattered here and there. Weather wise it was a gorgeous day with barely a cloud in the sky and it was gradually getting warmer inside carriage 463. On checking the long-range weather forecast, before leaving the UK, there were two warnings for extreme weather in Serbia and Croatia and on this day, it was estimated to go as high as 31 degrees across the region. The Balkan had no air conditioning, at least all the windows worked. Therefore, it would not be too unpleasant.

We reached Kalotina on the Serbian border before noon for the obligatory passport check. As these checks can take up to a good 30 minutes, I thought I would get off as I did many times before, stretch my legs, and have a vape.

Kalotina train station sits on the side of a Mountain and the Police post looks down on to the tracks so I caught sight of a Policeman watching me from above and I nodded to him and waived my vape to see if it was ok and he nodded back. So, I took the nod for smoking was ok. Isaac then got off the train and lit up a cigarette. We had a nice conversation about what he did and where he came from, which was Farnborough. I told him I knew the area well, which surprised him. After, I explained I had been in the Scots Guards, and trained at Pirbright, he understood. Anyhow, we were enjoying the sunshine, when the passport officer came along and shouted at Isaac for smoking, he never said a word to me. He ushered both of us back onto the train then I fluffed about the head nodding difference again. The police officer standing at the post was not nodding 'yes' it was a Bulgarian 'no'!

We got our passports back and a few minutes later, we were off again. However, we were not long in leaving Kalotina when the train arrived at Dimitrovgrad in Serbia. Another couple of passengers came onboard, then the train headed into the Pirotski region of south-eastern Serbia. After passing Pirot the Balkan slowed right down to almost a walking pace as it followed the Nisava River and into the Sićevo gorge. Isaac and I opened the back door to capture the view of the train going through the mountain tunnels.

They built the line in the 1880s and it was reminiscent of something you would see in an old western film. Especially, with the way the train was swerving and weaving along this single-track line. Sometimes it was just inches away from a sheer drop into the Nisava River. The scenery was breathtaking; I have never experienced a train journey like this before. I have never hung out the backdoor of a train before, and it did not seem dangerous at all given the snail like speed the train was going at. However, the best part about it was how refreshing it was, as the further, we got into Serbia the warmer and warmer it was getting.

As we came through the other side of the Sićevo gorge, the train gained speed and from the map, our next stop was at a place called Nis. I suspected that we would probably change over engines from the Bulgarian one to a Serbian ZS type as Nis was a major railway station. Better still, I could get off, stretch my legs, and get some fresh air.

Like Sofia, Nis is one of the oldest cities in Europe they also built it on top of an old Roman city. In addition, like the rest of Serbia, the Ottomans once ruled it. Interestingly, during WW1, it was the wartime capital of Serbia and during WW2; an SS German Division occupied it. During the Balkan Wars of the late 1990s, NATO cluster bombed it. So, there was a lot of history in this city, and sadly, I was not stopping off to visit it. For me it was just the beginning of the real Serbia and just another stop on my way to Belgrade.

As we approached Nis, you could see that it was an industrial city and since leaving Dimitrovgrad it was probably, the most heavily populated place I had seen on the route. When the Balkan pulled into the station, you could tell that it was definitely an international hub. There was rolling stock of all makes and sizes heading off in all directions across Europe.

This part of my journey was turning out to be one of the best, purely because of the scenery. Going through the Sićevo gorge was a wonderful experience. Also, it interested me that the Simplon Orient express had followed the same route at some stage. However, the downside was that the heat was reaching its peak. The carriage was beginning to feel like an oven, and my morale was slowly dwindling. The upside was Nis to Belgrade, was only 201 km away, not far really, yet it would take the Balkan just under five hours to get there.

I was expecting the Balkan to arrive in Belgrade at 6.18pm, but it trundled in at 7.45pm, which was irritating. I was expecting to have a full night in Belgrade. The train came to a stop at Topcider Train station a few miles south of the City Centre. I was hesitant about getting off as I understood the Balkan was going all the way into Belgrade's central station just down the hill from the Hotel Moskva. However, after being waved off the train I discovered that the Main Train station noted for the Orient Express stopover was closed; the Serbs had turned it into a Museum.

Trains going to Zagreb and other parts of the former Yugoslavia now went from another newly developed central station. It was all a tad confusing.

Topcider, station is a historical station in its own right. Built in 1884 to handle the visitors to the beautiful Topcider Park it has an interesting history. The park was the infamous spot where Pavle Radovanovic murdered the unpopular and possibly incestuous Prince Michael of Serbia in 1869. They taught the ill-fated King of Serbia Alexander Obrenovitch to swim there. Serbian military officers of the Black Hand Secret Society murdered the King in 1903. They also executed and mutilated Queen Draga in their chambers at the Old Palace. So, in the end I was not that disappointed about arriving in such a place of historical interest.

When we got off the train, it was a beautiful summers evening, and the Park was hosting some sort of event so there was many people around and there was a particular atmosphere about the place that made it appealing to be in the Serbian capital also known as the 'White City'.

The only public transport to go from Topcider Park to

Belgrade central was a tram and as I had no Serbian Dinars on me, I approached the taxi driver with the best-looking car. He looked like a cross between the American 1960s singer Frankie Valli and the medieval tyrant Vlad the Impaler. I asked him 'how much to Hotel Moskva' and he responded '15 Euro to Hotel Moskva'. Also, as Isaac, and Summer were staying in the city Centre I invited them to share my taxi. So, I told the taxi driver 'these two need to go to the Goodnight Grooves Hostel' he then said 'it will cost 20 Euro'. That was roughly twenty pounds, it was a lot for a taxi ride. However, after being on a train for nearly ten hours I would have offered him a lot more, I direly needed a shower and some refreshment.

Dick Turpin as I now called him, after the highway robber, took us off to Belgrade City Centre in his air conned immaculate C-Class Mercedes and gave us a half Serbian half English running description of Belgrade. On arriving at the City Centre, he dropped Isaac and Summer off at their hostel and then dropped me off a further 50 meters outside the impressive 4-star Hotel Moskva. The taxi driver seemed very happy when I handed over the 20 Euros and never even looked for a tip. If he did, he would have been out of luck as I had no small change.

After reading Le Corbusier's view and Rebecca West's description of Belgrade I was unsure on how I would find the place. I had witnessed the televised Balkan War of the 1990s and fully knew of the NATO bombing of the place, specifically the bombing of the Chinese Embassy in New Belgrade. The CIA had accidentally mistaken the Embassy for a Yugoslav Defence target, and hit the place with 5 bombs, which killed three journalists. So, I was conscious not to mention the war and if I got into a conversation with a Serbian, I would not dare to mention I was once in the British Army. I was later informed that the younger generation had largely forgotten the war, and that

NATO's involvement was seen as a purely political affair rather than one of hatred towards Serbs per se!

My raison d'être for adding Belgrade to my trip was because of my research for my book *Unauthorised Disclosure: British Military Traitors of the Cold War*. I had been researching the background of a Soviet KGB officer named Kuznetsov, who served in Belgrade between 1963 and 1970, and I had followed his postings around the world after he was expelled from the UK in the 1950s. So, I wanted to get a good feel for the place and its history. I wanted to stay in the Hotel Moskva (Moscow) it was the most famous Hotel in Belgrade if not the whole of Serbia.

The Moskva had a dark and interesting past. Its dark side is attributed to the Nazi occupation of Serbia, which the Nazi's codenamed 'Operation Punishment'. After Belgrade capitulated in 1941 the Gestapo requisitioned the Moskva and turned it into its Headquarters. Mikhail Kalashnikov the inventor of the infamous AK47 the preferred weapon of international terrorists had once stayed there, and the purchaser of such weapons Muammar Gaddafi had done deals there. So, in effect this Grand Dame once hosted the merchants of death. On the interesting side a horde of 'A' list movie stars such as Audrey Hepburn, Robert De Niro, and Pierce Brosnan, to name, but a few had all stayed there, including the movie producer Alfred Hitchcock. Political guests included Trotsky, Brezhnev, Yasser Arafat, and Richard Nixon. Even Frank Sinatra has graced its bedrooms. The visitor list is endless, and their photos are displayed throughout the hallways. More interestingly for me Rebecca West had lodged there during her visit to Yugoslavia between the wars. Also, another favourite author of mine and friend of Kim Philby, Graham Greene stayed there for four days in 1957.

The Swiss-French Architect Le Corbusier wrote, 'Belgrade was the ugliest city in the world, but in the most beautiful place in the world'. On first impression, Belgrade did not look that shabby. Likewise, after reading Rebecca West's *Black Lamb and Grey Falcon*, particularly the potted history of Serbia and Belgrade I guess I had formed a romantic view of the place. Besides, one needs to understand that Serbia's history is complex; it has the unfortunate label of being the most bombed city in the world. According to Rail Europe's website, it has been destroyed and rebuilt no less than forty times. So, Serbia has seen its fair share of war I estimated around one hundred and fifteen. As Rebecca West stated, 'Belgrade's history it is like many other passages in the life of Europe, makes one wonder what the human race has lost by its habit of bleeding itself like a mad medieval surgeon'.

After checking in to the Moskva, they showed me to the lobby lift as my room was on the fourth floor. As I was going up in the lift, I noticed a warning sign that prohibited the use of firearms, grenades, and Alsatians in the hotel, not something; you see every day in a British hotel.

My single bedroom was small, yet it was immaculately furnished and the view from the window was superb. It looked straight over the Terazijska Park, and it was getting dark, so I could not see much more than the lights of Belgrade. As time was moving on, I quickly got out of the sweaty clothes I had been travelling in all day and took a refreshing shower. The change in clothes felt great, and I was ready to sample the delights of the White City. I had arranged to meet Isaac and Summer for drinks at a place just around the corner on the famous Balkanska Street called Samo Privo, it was a Craft Beer pub, and it was supposed to be one of the best in Belgrade.

Unfortunately, Samo Privo only accepted cash. Serbia uses the 'Dinar' as a currency. So, I needed to get some out of a bank, but to my horror, I found none of my bankcards worked in all the ATM's I could find. Also, the Panther Money exchange shop next door to the Moskva was closed. It left me with no option, but to make an about turn and head back to the Moskva and use their bar. I could charge the drinks to my room. I sent Isaac and Summer a text to explain my plans had changed and to come and meet me at the hotel.

The terrace outside of the Moskva was very busy for a Sunday evening. But I found a great table looking on to Terazije Square. It was a great spot to sit and watch the Serbians go up and down this historic thoroughfare. Isaac and Summer eventually found me and we ordered a few drinks and as Isaac had ran out of cigarettes, we got cigars and sat like Kings and Queens drinking and smoking outside Serbia's most famous secessionist hotel.

The night went way too quick, and we finished being the last people to leave the terrace, which is not always a good impression to give. However, had the staff known what we had been through during the day I am sure they would have forgiven us. By now, we were all ravenous, so we headed to the MacDonald's across the way, and Isaac bought me a cheese-burger in recompense for the taxi fare. Eating a MacDonald's across the road from my 4 Star Hotel was not really how I wished my evening in Belgrade to end. Besides everything else was closed. Unbeknown to me the MacDonald's in Belgrade is supposed to be the biggest in the Balkans, a useless fact I know!

After eating the burger, we felt the night was still young, so we got takeaway beers from a nightstand next to Terazijska Park. This sloping park is right across from the Moskva and formed part of the Sava Ridge and apparently has wonderful views across the Sava Valley. So, we sat on a park bench chewing the fat until about 1 am. Then the Serb Police turned up and looked us over I acknowledged their stare and had a brief chat with them explaining our day and our travels, they seemed to understand us and left us alone. I eventually got to my bed about 2am I was exhausted and plummeted straight into a deep sleep.

My alarm went off around 7am. My train to Zagreb was due to leave at 10.20am so I had plenty of time to get ready and sort myself out for another days adventure. After I got showered and dressed, I sat at the room window staring out at New Belgrade and a across the valley towards the Sava River. The sky was grey, yet the city looked charming from that height. The view convinced me that Beograd is a place I will revisit soon.

I had breakfast on the Moskva's outside terrace and it was of a high standard. There was an excellent choice of food on display that catered for all types. I liked that they put on French toast a favourite dish, and one I do not have very often. But on this occasion, I helped myself to three slices, along with a large bowl of yoghurt, and two bananas. I thought this would see me through the day ahead. After, a couple of cups of coffee on the terrace I watched for the Panther money exchange shop to open as I needed to exchange some Euros for Serbian Dinars for my taxi, as I was not prepared to pay another 20 Euros. Also, I needed small change for supplies and my seat reservation for Zagreb.

The Panther exchange was right next-door to the Moskva, and I giggled to myself as I stepped through its doors. If you know anything about the Balkans recent past, you may have heard of the 'Pink Panthers'. They were or are a highly organised gang of jewel thieves who carried out high profile jewellery robberies all around the world during the early 2000s. The British press named them the Pink Panthers after the comedy film starring Peter Sellars. Because, they robbed Graff, the diamond specialists in London's New Bond Street of a £500,000 diamond then hid it in a jar of face cream. Apparently, it was very similar to a sketch in the movie *Return of the Pink Panther*.

The Panthers have been attributed with carrying out one

hundred and fifty-two robberies. By all accounts the profits from them were laundered in Belgrade via cafés, restaurants, and property.   So, here, I was in Belgrade exchanging Euros for Dinars in a shop called Panther Exchange, wondering if it is associated with the gang, but it is most definitely not!

View from the back door - Sicevo Gorge

The Hotel Moskva (Moscow), Belgrade

11

THE SAUNA TRAIN

The Concierge at the Moskva arranged for a taxi to pick me up and drop me off at the new Belgrade Central station known as Prokop. The cost was 400 Dinar the equivalent of about three British pounds. Dick Turpin the Mercedes Taxi driver had clearly done well out of me the night before.

Prokop is a strange station, no grand entrance, and no central concourse. It is like a train station built into a bunker. Albeit, it is still in the middle of being built.

In fact, on looking up the history of the station, it has been under development for almost thirty years. The place still does not even have a roof. To get to the platforms you descend from the street down a series of stairs until you get to the bottom. The platform I ended up on was the one I would leave from. So, all I had to do was find the International Ticket office, which was easy as it was in the middle of the same platform. The office was busy with a lot of backpackers and commuters sitting about all mainly heading to Croatia.

The middle-aged lady behind the counter had a name badge telling me her name was 'Odel'. So, I said to her 'Zdravo Odel, do you speak English', she replied back 'yes' in good English with a heavy slavic accent. I asked her if I needed a reservation for Zagreb, she explained that it is compulsory. The cost of the reservation was just 358 Dinars, a little less than the taxi ride I just had from the Moskva. Odel printed off my reservation grinned then told me that the train is very comfortable, and who knows if the air con will work or not? At that moment, I never understood the significance of that comment as the majority of the trains I had been on from Budapest to Bulgaria were mainly couchettes and none of them had air con except for an open window. I grinned back and told her I was looking forward to the trip and that I had enjoyed my stay in Belgrade.

After the journey from Sofia and the heat I encountered on board the Balkan, it was vital I stocked up with as much water as I could carry. I wandered around Prokop looking for a shop, but it looked like they had not got around to building one yet. The only facility selling water were vending machines, and when I found them, they were being restocked. So, at least there was plenty of bottles and other drinks available.

I found that I had exchanged too much money at the Panther Exchange, so I had plenty of Dinars left over. Exchanging them for Croatian Kuna's would be a waste of time so; I had to get rid of them. I looked at the selection of snacks and drinks within the vending machine and thought I should be able to spend everything I have on that. With an eight-hour journey ahead of me a ready supply of water, pretzels, and peanuts would not be a bad thing.

After a few minutes of hogging the machine, my activities attracted the attention of a kid who must have thought I was robbing it. He stood right next to me watching my every move. Because of him staring at me, I pushed the wrong buttons and got a pack of peanut flavoured crisps, which I knew would taste disgusting so I thought I would offer them to the kid in the hope he would go away. Without hesitation, he snatched them straight out of my hand and went back to his Mum and Dad. Then all off a sudden his Mother came over to me and started ranting in Serbian. I never understood what she was talking about, but I got the gist it upset her I had given her kid a pack of crisps. I apologised and tried to explain I bought them by mistake and rather than go to waste I thought the kid might like them? Her husband on hearing me speak English came over and told me in English they teach their kids not to accept things from strangers, however he thanked me for my kindness. Again, I apologised and then he walked away; it was the end of the affair, and it was a lesson learnt. On reflection, I should have just left the crisps on top of the machine for someone else to discover them.

The train turned up right on time it was a long train with a blend of Serbian EuroCity cars and other rolling stock. Compared to the Bulgarian trains, it looked modern. I found my coach and my seat was right by the door, which was handy. I could get off and on in between stops for a quick vape. The seat was also a recliner, which was a bonus. It looked like it would be a comfortable trip out of Belgrade and across the Pannonian plain.

The route I was about to embark on was a historic one. It goes right across the old Yugoslavia on the same track the Simplon Orient Express took, not to be confused with the Orient Express.

The Simplon route is where Agatha Christie's *Murder on the Orient Express* takes place. The difference in Orient Expresses is the Simplon used to go from Calais and Paris Gare de Lyon to Milan, Venice, Trieste, Zagreb, Belgrade, Sofia and Istanbul, whereas the Orient Express went from Paris Gare de l'Est via Munich, Vienna and Budapest. By this stage I had travelled on both routes at some stage on my journey.

Tim Vine's joke keeps ringing in my head 'mind you the Eurostar is comfy, but it is murder on the Orient Express isn't it'.

The official name of the train is the EuroNight 414 some call it the 'Alpine Pearl' because after Zagreb it changes into an overnight train, which passes through the Alps and ends at Zurich. For the majority of the route the 414 would follow the Sava River.

The Sava is one of the most important rivers in Europe because of its natural floodplain. It also connects three capital cities together, Belgrade, Zagreb, and Ljubljana in Slovenia. Like the early part of my journey where I followed the Danube all the way to Bulgaria, the Sava would be constantly nearby as I headed towards Slovakia.

Indeed, the train was very busy so no wonder a reservation was compulsory. I settled into my reclining EuroCity chair, and then felt the air con coming on, which was nice as the long-range weather forecast predicted that today would be like the day before, boiling! I spotted a waiter down the aisle selling tea and coffee so there was a catering car attached to the 414, which was good to know. It seemed the further I headed back towards the west the trains became more sophisticated.

The 414 was comfortable, so I put some music on and got out the other book I had brought along for the journey Leszek Kołakowski's *Is God Happy: Selected Essays* . It explores communism, socialism, evil, and religion. A friend recommended it after reading Karl Popper's *The Open Society and Its Enemies.*

Leszek was a critic of Marxist theory, so the Polish censor had confiscated a lot of his essays during the 1960s and then his daughter released them in English in 2012 The book had a great review, especially from the *The Polish American Journal*

A remarkable book.... All the essays are thought provoking. The late Kolakowski was one of the most renowned twentieth century intellectuals and philosophers. He had written essays and books for over fifty years, some of which were banned by the Communist party. Today we now have the pleasure of reading them in English, with an excellent translation by his daughter.

The essays are a good start to understanding the philosophy of socialism during the Cold War. His theories on Marxism are interesting and still very relevant today. Of all the essays in the book, I concluded that my favourite one is *The Myth of Two Sides to Every Question;* it is well worth a read. Moreover, it will make you think about a lot of situations where the theory is applicable in today's society.

Also, Kołakowski's views on religion got me thinking about the different religious groups in the Balkans. As the train went past the villages and towns, I spotted different styles of churches. Specifically, as the train passed through the autonomous province of Vojvodina. It is a self-governing area of Serbia, which has its own government including President. The political parties that govern the province are Serbian and Hungarian. Which explains why I saw Serbian Orthodox churches, a Romanian Orthodox Church and a Hungarian Catholic Church, or it could have been a Hungarian Greek Catholic Church I am not sure? It was later explained to me that the Serbian Orthodox Church is the second oldest Slav church in the world making Orthodox Christianity the dominant religion in the region.

The train stopped at Sremska Mitrovicka a city close to the Croatian border. It is the site of Serbia's biggest prison, and once a notorious Croatian Prisoner of War Camp during the Balkans war. Apart from its dark penal past I had read about the place when I studied Roman History. I knew during the Roman occupation of the province of Pannonia; they called it Sirmium. It was a place of significant historical importance and one of the four capitals of the Roman Empire.

Sremska Mitrovicka is a gold mine for Roman historians. I never thought I would travel through it when I was planning my trip. The remains of a Roman Imperial Palace are in this city; and I would have loved to have seen it. However, as I wrote at the beginning, everything between Belgrade and Bratislava was an enigma. As the train pulled away another Roman historical, thought crossed my mind. The Croatian born Emperor Diocletian who executed the Christian boy St Pancras (I mentioned him at the beginning of this book) was in charge of the province at one stage.

Some people who got on board at Sremska Mitrovicka were waving at elderly relatives on the platform. I wondered if they were Serbs living in Croatia and their families' had been pre-war Croatian Serbs who moved back because of the war. I find demographics interesting and being in a region that went through a very serious ethnic conflict made it more interesting.

Šid is the last major stop on the Serbian side. The Serbian Police came on board carried out a thorough search of the train and I mean every nook and cranny. I thought they were looking for drugs or weapons, I was later told they were looking for illegal immigrants.

As the train moved across the Pannonian plain, I noticed a big difference in the landscape compared to Bulgaria. It is like a tapestry, one minute there are green lush meadows, then the next minute there are vast flat fields full of Sunflowers and corn. They arrange the Sunflowers in columns like battalions of Guardsmen all standing tall about six feet in the air as far as the eye can see. It was a magnificent sight!

In contrast when the train crossed the border into eastern Croatia, the landscape changed again it became lusher and the houses looked more lavish, with swimming pools in the gardens and 4 x 4's in the driveway. Croatian farmers were no doubt finding things far easier than their Serbian counterparts were.

As the train passed through Sisak-Moslavina county, I noticed that it was becoming warmer in the carriage. It felt as if someone had turned the air con off as soon as the train was in Croatia. I put my hand down by my feet to feel for the air that had been keeping them cool and there was nothing coming in, on checking the top air vent, again I could not feel any air passing through? The windows were sealed so there was no way of letting to air in. It was becoming apparent that something was very wrong.

The heat was increasing minute by minute and I was not the only one who had noticed the change. There were people fanning themselves and some were moaning as if to say they were dying with the heat. I broke out into a sweat and decided it was time to take in lots of water. According, to my iPhone the temperature outside the train was close to 32 degrees Celsius. I got my towel out of my backpack and used it to block the sun coming in from the window and to soak up the gallons of sweat now pouring off me. I recall thinking at the time I am now travelling in a mobile Sauna! Moreover, Odel's statement about the air con came flooding back. She must have known that the air con would pack up due to the abnormal heatwave? I thought to myself so much for having a comfortable trip I am going to be cooked alive unless the train stops! A quick check of Google told me we were not far away from Vinkovic and the train must stop there!

The Sauna train did indeed stop at Vinkovic, which is ironic. In Agatha Christie's novel, it is the place, where the Orient Express stopped, and the murder of Samuel Ratchett took place. I remember thinking if they do not fix the air con there will be another murder! Everyone, got off the train to breathe and cool down in the shade. Electrical engineers went on board to look at the electrics, and after about forty minutes tinkering away they looked baffled. The system was kaput. By this stage all the passengers were complaining to the railway staff, the engineers had no choice, but to take the car out of service. Luckily, Vinkovic is the second biggest railway junction in Croatia so there was plenty spare rolling stock around. They replaced my carriage with a couchette and told everyone to find a seat on that. I just followed the crowd like a lost lamb. The compartment was full, but I got a seat by the door and I was relieved when I saw all windows were open.

After spending roughly one hour at Vinkovic the EuroNight took off. There were five more stations before Zagreb. One of which was Slavonski Brod, known as Brod. Another station mentioned in Agatha Christie's novel as the place where Hercule Poirot got off the Orient Express after solving the Ratchett murder.

As the train went through Sisak-Moslavina County, it rained, this broke the intensity of the heat for a while. By the time the train had reached the county of Zagreb it was early evening, and it had cooled down. It was turning out to be the perfect summers evening for a night out in Croatia's capital.

Glavni Kolodvor Station, Zagreb

12

ZDRAVO ZAGREB

Zagreb's historic Glavni kolodvor station was a welcoming site albeit the train was forty minutes late getting in. I was not fussed I was just glad to get off the Sauna train.

As you leave the central station, you hit King Tomislav Square, which is very impressive with its bronze statue of the first Croatian King. Originally, the square was named after Franz Joseph I the Emperor of Austria, King of Hungary, Croatia, and Bohemia. After World War I and the fall of the Austro-Hungarian Empire, they renamed it after King Tomislav.

Discovering the history surrounding the renaming of places because of fallen empires or government changes was turning into the norm. It made the region more fascinating. Despite the fall of the Austro-Hungarian Empire, you could see its influence in every direction. It was no surprise why the Croats wanted independence. The place looks grand and extravagant. It may be smaller than Paris or London, yet it is on a par with both, and it looks cleaner than both.

If you are a fan of *Murder on the Orient Express*, you can stay in the opulent Esplanade Hotel near the station. It was specifically built in 1925 to cater for passengers from the train. Similar, to the Hotel Moskva the list of wealthy and famous visitors is numerous and long. I however had booked a room in Zagreb's oldest standing hotel the Jagerhorn. Built in 1827 and with only eighteen rooms this little gem of a hotel is very much thought of within Croatian culture. They mention it in films, poems, and theatrical plays. Also, it has a long historical association with some of Croatia's leading players such as the Ban (Viceroy) Josip Jelacic, and the linguist Ljudevit Gaj (Ludwig Gay).

The history behind this little hotel was impressive. Finding it was comparatively straightforward, I got on a super new tram and got off two stops later at Ban Jelačić Square, which is the main square in Zagreb and from there it was 200 meters walk to the hotel. The Jagerhorn sits just off the pedestrian area and from its rear garden; you can walk up the back stairs to the Gothic style St Mark's church and square. Therefore, it was an excellent place for exploring the old town known locally as Gornji grad.

The hotel looks like a traditional hunting lodge inside and an old mews on the outside, it is lovely and it is very comfortable. The room was big and of a high standard. Having spent the last ten hours travelling my priority was to head straight into the shower, get rid of the dried up sweat from the Sauna train, and get into a set of fresh clothes!

After freshening up, I was buzzing with energy and could not wait to hit Zagreb.

Tkalčićeva Street commonly referred to as Tkalča by the locals is in the popular pedestrianized zone of the old town and it was a short walk from the Jagerhorn. This street was once famous for its Brothels, specifically the Kod Zelene Lampe (Green Lantern). Today they know it for its diverse range of restaurants, art shops and watering holes, it is a must place to go if you ever visit Zagreb!

I took a seat outside the All Saints restaurant under the shadow of St Mary's at Dolac church. It was a gorgeous evening and Tkalčićeva Street is that one place you can just relax, listen to good music, and watch Italian, German, and British tourists walk past enjoying themselves.

As it got darker, hunger took over, and I moved off in search of some food further up Gornji grad. As I wandered past all the bars and restaurants, I suddenly came across a Greek restaurant that looked interesting. I had eaten a lot of chicken on my trip so I was not looking for more; I was looking for some seafood for a change. However, on surveying El Greco's menu I spotted Gyros a dish I had not eaten since I left Germany in 1993. It is spicy pork meat roasted on a spit, and when you mix it with tzatziki sauce, onions, and pitta bread, it makes one tasty meal. It was a must have!

As I devoured the Gyros, knocked back the beer I analysed the day's trip, specifically my low morale on the Sauna train. Nevertheless, Zagreb brought out a sense of deep joy. It was a place that just made you feel good.

As I sat, there outside El Greco's sipping the last drops of my beer an elderly woman approached my table and cleared up the empty plastic bottles and cans. At first, I thought she worked for the restaurant and then when the waiter came out, he nodded to her and told her it was ok. It then struck me she was not working at the restaurant at all; she was collecting the bottles and cans for herself. I asked her if she spoke English, and she nodded no then in Croatian, she said, she spoke a little German. So, I asked her in my limited German if she was recycling the bottles; she replied 'nicht' and explained that she takes the bottles and cans to get the money back on them. I found out from a friend who lives in Bosnia that the old folk collect the bottles because it supplements their meagre pensions. My heart sank, I asked her what age she was, and she told me 'dreiundachtzig' she was 83. It astonished me that a woman of her age was out so late doing that in a place that looks like it is prospering!

That is the reality of life. It is not always what it seems. Anyway, my night in Zagreb went way too quick and it was time for my bed. I headed back down the street towards St Mary's, then I saw the elderly woman at another table on the Tkalča. Something inside of me made me go over to her and place sixty Croatian Kuna in her hand, I then said to her 'Auf Wiedersehen'. She was delighted and accepted the money. I guess it was a combination of reading Kołakowski, being slightly inebriated, and feeling sorry for her that urged me to give her something. I hope it lifted her spirits up and things change in Croatia. The government needs to take better care of its pensioners!

Tomislav Square, Zagreb

Gornji grad, Zagreb

13

DOVIĐENJA ZAGREB

I got up at 6am, as my train from Glavni kolodvor was leaving at 7.25am. I wanted to get to the station in plenty of time to explore the place and get some snacks for the five-hour journey to Vienna.

As I was leaving the Jagerhorn, the receptionist stopped me. She said 'Mr Gorman as you are not staying for breakfast, we took the courtesy of preparing one you can take away with you'. I thought 'wow' how very decent of them. It was definitely a fitting end to my short stay in the historic Jagerhorn and Zagreb. I felt saddened that I had not spent more time doing my homework on Zagreb, as I would have loved to have stopped another day and night. That said, Zagreb was not important to my research. It was just on the way and had looked the ideal place to stop and break up the journey.

I took the tram back down to the Tomislav square and found a little newsagent to stock up with titbits. After wandering around the station looking at its neoclassical architecture, I went in search of the platform that would take me out of Croatia. Today's route would take me right across Slovenia and up through Austria to Vienna.

Getting to Vienna from Zagreb is simple there are four Euro-City trains a day, all modern couchette style, which I was becoming fond off. Most trains to Austria leave from platform 4, which is easy to find, yet some people get mixed up with the 'A' and 'B' part. When I turned up on the platform, it looked simple. The train on platform 'A' was a EuroCity train and the one on platform 'B' was a local train.

As usual, I got on board and found my compartment. On entering it looked full, because there were three teenagers sprawled all over the place and a fellow with a lot of crucifixes around his neck stuck in the corner. I thought to myself this will be fun!

I had to ask one teenager to get out of my seat as again I had booked a window seat. As she got up, I got that typical teenager look of contempt followed by a sigh. When I sat down the guy with the crucifixes smiled at me as if to say 'well done' or perhaps he was happy that another adult was sharing the compartment?

After, I was settled, I tucked into the Jagerhorn breakfast, which was two small rolls with ham, a carton of soft cheese, blueberry yoghurt and a banana, it was all solid food to get me through to Vienna. On munching my way through the break-fast, whilst gazing out of the window, I noticed an old man going through the rubbish bins collecting plastic bottles. Suddenly, I thought about the elderly woman I had met the night before and felt disheartened. I thought, it is more widespread than I first thought. Life is very unfair, and I cannot change Croatia's' socially unbalanced situation.

As the EuroCity left Glavni kolodvor the fellow sat across from me introduced himself in German and I informed him in German that my Deutsch was very limited, so he responded in English. He told me he was from Dresden and had been travel-ling for a week around the Balkans. Given the number of crucifixes he was wearing I was dying to ask him if he had been to Bran Castle in Brasov and were the crucifixes protection from Vampires, but I thought better. I did not think he would see the humour in it. The three teenagers turned out to be from Spain, and looked, and acted like gap year students on a Euro trip. Their kit was strewn all over the place. Also, by the look on their faces they must have been partying hard the night before; one thing is for certain they looked shattered. I thought they will all be asleep shortly and it will be peaceful trip.

Once you leave Zagreb for Vienna, the Slovenian border is not that far away and before you realise it you are in a different world. An alpine world with beautiful forests and the Sava River flowing right next to you. I had never considered staying in Slovenia when I planned the trip, and it was fast growing into a regret, as the place is just stunning.

After two hours of sitting in the same coach as the Spanish teenagers they were getting on my nerves, it was like being in a youth hostel with their sleeping bags strewn out across the floor and with their feet up on the seats. I just wanted some peace and quiet. So, I walked down the carriage and found an empty couchette and relocated to that.

The ride through Slovenia was short and before you know it, you are at the Austrian border. The Police and Austrian Army came on board to check everyone's passports. I got off for a quick vape and to have a look at the border crossing point. The Army manned it, no doubt because of the migrant crisis that took place in 2017. The crisis had affected the whole region due to the proximity of Greece to Central Europe.

The delay at the border was longer than expected, and when the train took off it passed through the old Duchy of Styria. The scenery as you head towards Graz is breathtakingly beautiful. Rolling hills and alpine mountains it was no surprise why they call it the 'Green Heart of Austria'. However, despite the beauty of Styria the delay at the border caused the train to be behind schedule. So, it meant I would arrive in Vienna at 2.08pm. That only gave me five minutes to find my platform and catch the 2.13pm to Košice.

Having never been in the new Vienna train station before and with no idea of how the platforms where laid out I could feel anxiety building up inside me. So, far I had not missed a connection, and I did not want to miss the one to Slovakia. Although, the train to Slovakia ran every hour so missing it would not have been a total disaster it was just a matter of principle. I had taken pride in getting this far and meeting all my connections. Missing one at this stage would have been disappointing, and it was fast becoming a probability.

You expect delays on the eastern networks because the infrastructure is a lot older than the western one. Also, the Austrian and German railway systems pride themselves on efficiency. So, I never expected delays on this part of my journey. I guess at this stage felt I was developing some form of train OCD. Furthermore, as the train reached the outskirts of Vienna my worst fear was turning into a reality.

The EuroCity halted at Vienna exactly at 2.08pm. I now had to find the platform for Košice, easy enough if you know your way around Vienna Hauptbanhoff. I ran to the central concourse and scanned the departure board for Košice and it was leaving from platform 8. I saw the stairs to the platform and sprinted towards them barging past Austrian commuters going about their daily business. As I got to the top of the stairs, I ran for the first door I could find then I heard the platform guard blow the whistle. Luckily, the train was a Slovakian one, and the doors were not automatic. I made it with seconds to spare.

As soon as I got the pack off my back, the train took off. I opened the door to the carriage and found myself in the catering one. It was very 1970s looking, but it was ideal for the one-hour trip to Slovakia.

Admittedly, I was out of breath; I don't think I have ever run that fast for a train in my life. So, I breathed in and out then sank into the seat. The young Slovakian waiter, smirking like a Cheshire cat, looking smart in his white shirt, waistcoat and bowtie stared inquisitively at me from behind the bar. He did not understand what it meant for me to catch this specific train. I looked back at him then asked if he was open, he smirked and replied, 'what would you like'. I knew exactly what I wanted and without hesitation I asked for a Viennese coffee with the cream on top too!

I sat nursing my coffee looking at the countryside as the train crossed the Austro-Hungarian plain heading east towards Košice. My next stop was Bratislava just one hour away, it was the shortest train journey I had taken in the last eight days.

Bratislava was the mainstay of my trip; I had deliberately booked to spend two nights there to explore as much of it as I could and soak up all the Slovakian culture Bratislava offered.

As the EuroCity came out of the tunnel and slowed down to stop at Bratislava's Hlavná stanica, I wondered if a lot of the tourists on their way to Košice, Prague, and Vienna knew the significance of the tunnel they had just passed through, and what was sitting underneath it?

Beautiful Slovenia

14

LITTLE BIG CITY

Hlavná stanica on the outside is an ugly station. The original station was built in 1848, and they rebuilt it in the 1960s in the socialist style. Sadly, it does not do Bratislava justice.

A lot of people visit Bratislava because of the Castle and the Old Town a lot of them have no idea of its military or secret past. Indeed, I would class Bratislava as an area of significant military importance.

Hlavná stanica station holds one secret apparently many young Slovakians do not know about. Built into the tunnel there is the entrance that leads down to a vast Cold War bunker. I guess the ignorance is similar to the World War Two deep-level shelters I walk past most days in Clapham, a lot of young people do not know they are there.

During the 1950s the Communists built a shelter under Hlavná stanica to house 1,500 citizens from air attacks and weapons of mass destruction. Built, with a command Centre, air filtering, toilets and generators to sustain it through a long-term attack. Slovakians who walk down Jaskovy rad Street every day on their way to work do not even know what is below their feet.

Unfortunately, it is not open to the public and I am led to believe Slovak Railways still maintain it in the event of another World War or conflict in that region.

My hotel was about two kilometers from the station. My original plan was to walk from the station to the hotel, but it was a hot day. I looked at taking a bus, yet I did not want to spend an hour trying to work out where each one was going then end up going the wrong way. So, I opted for the easiest choice and got a taxi. My track record so far with taxis was not good. However, the ones sitting outside Hlavná stanica were metered Taxis. I thought it would not cost that much to go about 2 kilometers. How wrong was I! As soon as I got in the taxi the driver set the meter to 20 Euro, I almost screamed 'are you sure that is the price to go 2 kilometers', the Slovakian driver smiled at me and said 'yes take it or leave it', hmm it was about 25 degrees outside and I had been traveling since 7.25am so I grumpily said 'ok let's go'.

The taxi driver dropped me off on Klemensova Ulica in the east part of the old town. The Elizabeth Hotel would be my bed for the next two nights. So, I gave the rip off taxi driver his 20 Euros. He smiled at his victory then tried to help me with my pack, I shrugged him off and told him I was fine and made him know in no uncertain terms he was a crook, whether he understood me I will never know.

So, my first introduction to Bratislava was a rip off taxi driver, it was not a great introduction I was livid. Dick Turpin the taxi driver in Belgrade who also charged me 20 Euros was a different case altogether as there were three of us and it was a longer trip, besides we had just got off a train after a hellish nine-hour journey. This time it was a very short journey and a very blatant tourist rip off. Anyway, I put it down to another lesson learnt.

The Elizabeth Hotel; is a cheap, and decent hotel on the outskirts of the historical Centre. Location wise, it is a five-minute walk to the Danube in one direction and a five-minute walk to the old town in the other. Perfect for my needs. The receptionist who sat behind a huge glass window, the type you saw in old banks gave me room 205, it was the same room number I had in Sofia at the Hotel Bristol. So, not only had I got the same seat number on different trains twice I now had the same room number in two different hotels. 56 and 205 were becoming my lucky numbers. However, the number 20 was proving to be a bad omen, well money wise it was.

The door to room 205 was heavily padded on both sides with a cheesy white leather, I had a chuckle to myself and thought maybe it was an old interrogation cell. Well the building looked as though it was an official building at some stage of its life. Nevertheless, if the door blocked the noise from the other guests it was a good thing.

I spent a few hours in my hotel room sorting clothing out and checking out I had everything for my trip back to London. About 6pm I wandered into the old town along Klemensova Ulica or Clemens Street. They named the street after Józef Božetech Klemens who was a painter, sculptor, and naturalist. So, I guessed I was in what you would describe as the Art district of Bratislava. The street had several culturally important buildings on it, and the eye-catching Church of St Elizabeth is situated just around the corner. The 'Blue Church' as it is commonly known, is a Hungarian Secessionist Catholic church painted Sky blue and beautifully done in the Art nouveau style, it is well worth a visit.

Many of the buildings on the street were built in the 1920s. But there is the odd 1950s communist style building slotted in between buildings, looking out of place with their ugly socialist facades. Maybe one day the Slovakian government will tear them down and rebuild something that fits in.

As I entered the historical part of the city, you could see why

Bratislava is very popular with tourists. The streets are narrow and cobbled. Some, of the buildings even date back to the medieval period. I was in search of the man in the hole called Cumil, 'The Watcher'. It is a bronze man watching the street from a manhole and he is very popular with the tourists. I was looking for him as I knew when I found him, I would be at the junction of Laurinská and Panská Ulica. I was looking for the street where the British Consulate is located, but I was not in need of consular advice I was looking for ZiL Verne, a craft beer pub 100 meters from the consulate, it was highly recommended to me as a pub that serves some of the best beer in Bratislava.

In fact, a good place to start in Bratislava is Panská Ulica as it is very lively, and you can sit and watch the world go by whilst sipping on an excellent beer.

A few beers later I went for a meal then ended up walking into an open-air live music show, which was drawing the crowds in. I must admit the band was good. The lead singer was from England and he was obviously heavily influenced by U2 and Queen as he pumped out some of their greatest hits. I stayed and listened to the music until they were finished then headed back towards Klemensova Street.

It was a very entertaining first night in Bratislava, and I could see why it is very popular with tourists. Good beer, good food and free outdoor music concerts.

The next day I got up about 9am and gave the Hotel breakfast a miss to try somewhere local. Klemensova Ulica had a few cafés on it, yet the one across from the Elizabeth looked nice plus it had outside seating.

The food in Kubistu's Bistro was a cross between Austrian and Hungarian and all locally sourced. The homemade sourdough bread was delicious and the coffee was excellent, it was good breakfast to start the day with.

My main aim for the morning was to get within two kilometers of Kittsee on the Slovakian - Austrian border. I was in search of a war relic not that well known to a lot of Slovakians never mind someone from the UK. A friend had told me about the place and suggested that I would find the place interesting, he had also given me clear instructions on how to get there.

The first part was to find the Kochova bus stop, which was about a twenty-minute walk from Klemensova. This part turned out to be easy, and it was a nice walk through the old town into the newer part of town. Along the way I walked past an official looking building with bars on the windows and on the wall, someone had spray painted the words *Do not fear the Ghost of Stalin* I had seen a lot of graffiti during my trip, and that was the most unusual one and the first one in English.

I found the bus stop right on the main Staromestská, which is a bypass which splits the old and new part of Bratislava apart. I was advised to buy a ticket that would be valid for about fifteen minutes. It was very similar to how it is done in Budapest and in most countries in the region. The ticket was very inexpensive and easy to buy. I was then told to get on a Number 80 bus, and that was not long in coming. The bus went over the Danube, across the impressive UFO bridge known as the bridge of the Slovak National Uprising (Most SNP). Once on the other side you are in the Petržalka district and close to the border with Austria.

Petržalka is an interesting district of Bratislava. The Germans annexed it in 1938, and it was the site of a Hungarian Jewish labour camp, where they forced the inmates to work on the Südostwall (South-East Wall). The fortification system built by the Germans towards the end of World War Two. I was looking for a fortification system, but not one built for the Germans by forced labour. The one I was looking for was built to keep the Germans out.

My instructions told me to get off at Kopčianska, and just

head straight down that road 'you will find it'. The instructions all seemed straightforward. So, I got off at Kopčianska before the bus turned left away from the main road. It seemed all I had to do now was walk straight down this main road and I would find what I was looking for. Anyway, I checked Google maps and saw I was still a few kilometers away from Kittsee. I then asked someone at a bus stop if they knew if a bus went towards Kittsee, but they shrugged their shoulders and looked at me as if I had just landed from the moon. At this point I thought about abandoning my search, however having got this far I decided to keep on going and started to walk down Kopčianska.

The surrounding area just resembled an industrial area on one side and a complex of communist built Panelak (panel building constructed of pre-fabricated, pre-stressed concrete) housing estates on the other. There was nothing to show I was near an international border, so I persevered and kept on walking.

After walking about two and a half kilometers I stopped and checked the map on my phone, again and there was still nothing showing up. There was nothing like I was told there would be. So, I rechecked the instructions I was given, and I had not deviated from them. At this stage it was approaching midafternoon and it was getting very hot, I reckoned it must have been about 22 degrees.

I walked for about another kilometer when I came across a busy flyover, which I suspected was the E65. It was one of the longest roads in Europe. It starts in Sweden and ends up in Greece. Then I spotted a compound with CCTV cameras around it. The brickwork on the walls looked very familiar, it was the same type I had seen on Russian barracks in East Germany. Also, the cameras suggested that it was a Government compound or some military facility. The dead giveaway that it was official was the signs on the gate 'Pozor' (Warning). So, when I saw that compound, I knew I could not be far from the old border. As I walked under the flyover and another couple of hundred meters, I saw a sign 'Bunker BS 8, 500 meters'. Bingo, I had found it.

Bunker system 8 was one of about nine bunkers built around Petržalka in the 1930s by the 4th Engineer Regiment from Bratislava. All, designed by General Josef Šnejdárek the Regional Military commander to defend Czechoslovakia from a German invasion.

General jiri Šnejdárek (Joseph Georges Schneidarek 1875-1945) was a remarkable soldier. He was a 28-year veteran of the French Foreign Legion and had seen active service in the First World War. A veteran of Verdun he successfully led the Czech army against the Hungarian Bolsheviks at Zvolen in Central Bratislava in 1919. He was still formally serving in the French Army at the time. His memoirs *What I have gone through* state he never 'lost a battle or a dual'. The history of the General can be found on the Wittman Holding family website.

BS-8 was the largest and most armed bunker in the series. Manned by a garrison of 33 men in its day. After the war it was absorbed into the Iron Curtain as it sat along the 'Pohraniciarska signalka' (Borderline signal).

I could not locate the official path to bunker so I followed a dirt track that looked like an old border route with what looked like the remains of a Tank berm at the side. Also, there was the odd bit of barbed wire poking out here and there. I found the official border road that led to a car park and the World War One Cemetery next to the Bunker. The route to that was just as mysterious as the route to BS-8 itself.

Local volunteers who do tours for the school kids and the odd tourist like me now staff the bunker. They have preserved its history well and it is well worth a visit if you are up for the long mysterious walk to find it.

The Military Cemetery that is adjacent to the Bunker was laid out in 1916 to intern casualties from the Austro-Hungarian Empire and its enemies. Astonishingly, there are soldiers from nine different nationalities buried in the cemetery, Czech, Hungarian, Yugoslav, Romanian, Austrian, Russian, Italian, Polish, and German. The majority of the 331 soldiers died in the Creation Hospital in Bratislava and some in the Divisional Hospital and Kopčany. Not all of them are named, and there is a few just marked 'Neznamy', which means 'unknown'.

After exploring BS-8 and stocking up on more water I strolled along the 'Pohraniciarska signalka' or Iron Curtain route all the way round until it hit the Kopcianska Ulica again. It was a nice walk and the views across the fields towards Austria were beautiful. On route you hit the odd sign Pozor – warning! Štátna hranica – state border. Do not cross! which takes you back in time to the Cold War. I couldn't believe this area of natural beauty was at one stage littered with mines and divided by an electric fence, with watchtowers and guard dogs.

According to a Cold War brochure I had with me, since 1948 and 1989 forty-two civilians had been killed trying to escape across the border.

On the road back I found Bunker 9, which was a smaller field bunker nowhere near as imposing as 8 and looked as though it would have been protected by two guards. By this stage, it was boiling and I was running out of water again. So, I headed back up Kopčianska in the direction I came from. On passing a lane I noticed a Police car so I approached them to ask if there was anywhere nearby, I could buy water. The two Policemen sitting in the car looked as though they were enjoying a break, as both doors were open and they were smoking away. As I approached them, I waved saying 'hi' and smiling 'do you speak English', they both looked at me in surprise and looking stunned both said 'no'. Then one said he spoke a little German, I sighed with relief and said, 'ah gut'. I asked them in my broken German if there was a 'Geschaft' anywhere nearby. The older policeman tried to explain there was a Supermarket about 3 kilometers in one direction, and in the other direction about two kilometers away there was a Pension (Guesthouse). I opted for the Pension and the 2-kilometer walk. As I headed off in the direction of the guesthouse, I wondered what the Policemen were thinking. I speculated if they might come and stop me just to find out what a Scotsman was doing in the middle of nowhere. They never came.

The Pension was tucked away off the road, and it was a relief to find it. I believe at that stage I was feeling dehydrated. Apart from a dry mouth, I was starting to get cramps in my legs and my skin was cool and dry. As I drew closer, I saw that all the windows had their shutters down, I thought just my luck they are closed. Then I noticed a door was open at the side of the building. So, I stepped inside to a pleasant cool reception room and was greeted by a particularly attractive looking Slovakian receptionist.

I said to her 'good afternoon do you speak English', she grinned and answered, 'I do how can I help', I responded 'do you sell anything to drink', she answered 'yes help yourself in the fridge behind you'. I bought two bottles of very chilled water then sat outside in the shade. After rehydrating myself I asked Kveta (her name means Flower of Blossom) the receptionist if she could get me taxi back to Klemensova Ulica. By now all I wanted was a good shower and a change of clothes.

After freshening up in the Elizabeth I headed back into the old town to visit the Grassalkovich Palace home of the President of Slovakia. They completed the Palace in 1760 in the baroque style. There is a changing of the Guard at 12 noon every day when the President is in residence, but I had missed that. However, it was nice to see the Palace returned to its original

splendour.   During the communist era they named it after
Klement Gottwald a zealous communist and ally of Stalin who
changed the Palace into the Bratislava House of Pioneers and
Youth.   The Bratislava young pioneers caused considerable
damage to the place and it was left in ruins until the Velvet
Revolution of 1989.

If you ever go to Bratislava, you will not miss or perhaps you
should not miss visiting St Michaels Tower.   It is the only
medieval gate left that once protected the city.   Built in the 14th
century then refurbished in the 18th century.   It is now a
weapons museum with seven floors and stunning views across
the old town.   This impressive gateway leads you on to a beautiful street with the same name and a good place to stop and
grab something to eat.

After devouring a schnitzel with pomme frites I wandered
down Michalská Ulica picking up souvenirs and taking photos.

For the final part of the evening I headed back to Panská
Ulica and took up a seat outside ZiL Verne's.   My last few hours
in Bratislava known as the 'Little Big City' was spent just
watching the world go by until it was time to head back to
Klemensova and bed.   It was a great two days in the Slovakian
capital.

Cumil (The Watcher)

The Blue Churh - St Elizabeth

Political graffiti in Kochova, Bratislava

Bunker BS-8, Kopcianska, Petrzalka

The Old Iron Curtain, Bratislava

St Michaels Gate, Bratislava

15

APFELSTRUDEL AT THE PALACE

O n my original schedule I had planned to get the train from Bratislava to Vienna at 7pm. However, I had seen and done everything I wanted to do in the Slovakian capital. So, I decided to head to Vienna early and spend a day in the Austrian capital.

As I booked out of the Hotel Elizabeth, I asked the staff to order me a taxi to the station and asked for a price. The receptionist told me it would only cost 8 Euros, which was a massive difference compared to my first journey there. The taxi was not long in coming so I said, 'goodbye' to the staff. Unlike the Bristol where I told the staff I would leave them a favourable review I never thought it was necessary with the Elizabeth. There was nothing outstanding about the place and they never suffered from a lack of trade so they will survive without my accolade.

As soon as I arrived at Hlavná stanica, there was a train about to leave for Vienna so I jumped on that and found a seat by the window. As I went through the tunnel with the Cold War bunker below me, I thought about a return trip to Slovakia. The train went past Devínska Nová Ves on the Austrian border and there is an abandoned Soviet Missile base ensconced on Devínska Kobyla Mountain that I never got to see. Also, there is the concrete pillar that marks the tripoint of the Slovakian, Austrian, and Hungarian, borders near the village of Čunovo. So, it is definitely worthy of another trip.

The train to Vienna was on board a rather boring Austrian City Shuttle, but at least it was a short journey. There are two different train routes to Vienna from Bratislava. One leaves every hour from Hlavná stanica, which goes North of the Danube and there is another, which leaves every two hours from Petržalka and goes South of the Danube. Luckily, I was on the Northern route so I would get to cross the Austrian part of the Danube near Donauinsel, which would be my last crossing of that magnificent river on this journey.

On arrival at Wien (Vienna) Hauptbanhoff and not in a hurry this time, I had time to look around. I would rate it as one of the best railway stations I have ever been in. With one hundred shops and restaurants it makes its counterparts in the east look very dated. They designed the station to accept trains coming from four different directions. So, it has 16 tracks and 15 platforms. It is an awesome feat of railway engineering and design.

The left luggage room is easy to find and easy to use. So, I left my backpack in the station and went out to explore the Austrian capital.

You cannot visit Vienna and not try Viennese Apple Strudel and coffee; it is the quintessential Austrian dish. There are plenty of places that serve the dish, but I wanted to end the last day of my journey in luxury. So, I opted for the Café Menagerie at the upper Belvedere Palace.

It was a beautiful morning in Vienna so I strolled along the

Wiedner Gurtel past Argentinier Strasse towards the Quartier Belvedere. I hit Prinz Eugen Strasse and then swung left down the hill towards the entrance to Schloss Belvedere.

They built the palace at the behest of Prince Eugene of Savoy (1663-1736) who was a very successful military commander. He was born in the Hôtel de Soissons Paris and was raised in the court of Louis the XIV. However, after being rejected for service in the French army he moved to Austria and swore allegiance to the Hapsburgs. He ended up fighting many battles against the French. Most notably he fought alongside the Duke of Marlborough, Sir Winston Churchill's ancestor at the Battle of Blenheim in 1704. Thus, saving Vienna from being captured by a Franco-Bavarian army.

As well as being a great soldier Eugene was a lover of the arts and a connoisseur of baroque architecture. The upper palace is now part of a grandiose complex of baroque style gardens with a lower palace. The place is now a Museum that houses many of Eugene's art collection. Café Menagerie is situated at the side of the palace, and it was a stunning location for a well-earned sumptuous brunch of vanilla ice cream, fresh cream, and warm apple strudel.

After brunch I went on a free wander around the palace art gallery, when I say free, I mean I asked to use the toilet. The toilets are on the other side of the gallery. So, you have to go through the halls and come back through them to get to the café, so I got a free tour.

With clear blue skies above, the view from the upper palace to the lower was beautiful. I walked through the palace botanical gardens down to the lower palace, Prince Eugene's official residence. He was so rich he could afford to build not only two palaces in Vienna, but three. The Winter Palace is in the old town.

Near to the lower palace there is the 'Heroes' Monument of the Red Army'. So, I went and paid that a visit. It is a vast colonnade of marble dedicated to the 17,000 Soviet soldiers who died liberating Vienna from the Nazis. The move by Stalin to capture Vienna was not only a tactical move, it was a political move, he thought he could use Vienna as a bargaining chip during the ensuing Allied control of the city. The Soviet Marshall Fyodor Tolbukhin (his railway carriage is housed at the Bulgarian Transport Museum in Russe) was in charge of the Soviet troops that captured Vienna, and it was not a glorious victory because of the amount of sexual assaults they committed against the female populace. No wonder the monument is vandalised from time to time.

The Kartner ring is a short walk from the Soviet War memorial and is part of a Ringstrasse aptly named the 'Lord of the Rings Roads', which goes around the old town. It is also a UNESCO World Heritage Site! The Ringstrasse leads you to the Vienna State Opera, Parliament, and many more places of cultural importance. Some say it is the most beautiful boulevard in the world and I would not disagree!

It was a pleasant walk up to the Vienna State Opera where I sat for a while and watched the world go by. After, watching Mozart lookalikes trying to sell Japanese tourists tickets for the Opera I headed back towards the train station. I wanted to find somewhere I could relax for a few hours. So, I headed down Karlsplatz and across the park towards another grand baroque building the Karlskirche Church or Karls Church. They consider this 18th century church one of Vienna's greatest buildings. Interestingly, the Knights of the Cross-with the Red Star who can trace their lineage back to the Crusades of the 13th century care for the church. It was also the church were the composer Gustav Mahler was married. I was in awe of its history and design and could have sat in the park gazing at it all day. However, there were a few drifters hanging about and the Police were patrolling the park. I decided to move on and find somewhere much more comfortable.

At the back of the church there begins the start of Argentinier Strasse, named in the 1920s after Argentina who donated 5 million to help Austria recover after the First World War. The street is very long and heads uphill towards the Wiedner Gurtel and the train station.

Along the way I found the Café Goldegg. It looked like an interesting and suitable place to hold up until my final move to the Hauptbanhoff.

Transport yourself back in time to the turn of the 20th century and you are in Café Goldegg. On reading up on its history, which is in the menu card, it tells you it is a listed protected café because of its Art Nouveau style decoration and original fittings. Founded in 1910 by the Viennese coffeehouse family Dobner it was a regular haunt for the railway workers, who came down the hill from the Hauptbanhoff, no doubt for a few beers and a meal. Until about 1941 when the Nazi's occupied Vienna it was the meeting place for persecuted trade unionists and revolutionary socialists. However, the café's history does not mention what happened to the socialists after 1941, one can only imagine.

After exploring the inside of Goldegg, I took up a seat on one of the tables outside. It was a glorious afternoon and there were a few locals sitting about enjoying the sunshine. As I was completing my daily diary, I could not help noticing that the two short haired athletic looking men who sat down on the table right next to mine started speaking in Russian. After, the journey I had been on looking at relics of the Cold War it sort of put a shiver down my spine. Then I remembered that there is a large Russian community in Vienna. Nevertheless, I still found it a tad spooky.

I spent my final two hours reading, writing and drinking coffee at this wonderful café then it was time to leave for the final leg of my journey.

Belvedere Palace, Vienna

The view from the rear of the Belvedere Palace

16

GOODNIGHT VIENNA

After settling my bill at Café Goldegg I headed up the hill to the impressive Wien Central station. As I entered the concourse, I stared up at the departure board, which was humongous, yet simple to follow. There were trains going everywhere it was incredible. If you wished you could get on a train all the way to Monaco in the South of France. It was tempting. However, I noticed that my train to Cologne was not listed, maybe because I was early.

I went to get my backpack from left luggage, and as I opened the locker door and reached up to grab it, I felt someone peeking over my shoulder. As I spun around it turned out to be a guy who suddenly begged me for some money. I thought to myself for goodness' sake leave me alone, I told him 'sorry I don't understand', and he responded in fluent English 'fifty cents for a coffee', so I flipped him one Euro and barged out of the way.

Sadly, train stations and by this stage I had been in a few are a magnet for many individuals, alcoholics, beggars, the homeless, pickpockets and no doubt other criminal elements. If you sit on a bench outside of a central train station and just watch, you can spot them all. I had become skillful in identifying those looking for an opportunity to extract money from a traveller. From outside St Pancras to Vienna I had seen it all. I had observed a woman go up the side of the station and urinate. I had seen homeless drunks fight over a small living space and I had watched the watchers looking for easy pickings. That is train stations for you.

So, on this final leg of my trip I had to get a NightJet train that would take me from the Danube to the Rhine. I rechecked the departure board and the only train I could see going towards the Rhineland was a train running to Dusseldorf. So, I headed to the OBB (Österreichische Bundesbahnen) office to ensure it was the correct train.

The last thing I needed was to get on the wrong train. To date everything had gone smoothly except for the delayed Zagreb train to Vienna, so I was hoping Vienna was not turning into a jinx. I asked the man behind the counter in the OBB office in my best German if he spoke English and he gave me a nod and sighed, I took that sigh as sign of do you not know everyone in Austria speaks English, even the beggars. I always found it polite to ask first. Nonetheless, I showed him my ticket, and he printed me off an itinerary of the NightJet 40490. It was going all the way to Dusseldorf via 13 different cities. I only had to get off at Koln.

The NightJet pulled into Vienna and the coach I was on stopped right in front of me. The train comprised a sleeping car; with deluxe and standard compartments that went up to 3 berths, a couchette car with up to six berths and a 2nd class coach with six seats per compartment. I was in a six-berth couchette car and it was packed to the gunnels. My reservation stated that I was on the upper bunk. This was something I was not looking forward to. I much prefer the bottom bunk, it is easier to get in and out of, especially if you need to use the toilet.

I was the first one to get in the couchette, and not far behind me was Albert an Austrian who worked in IT; he was going to Frankfurt. Then Chudy from California and her Mum Lou from Nevada who were both going on a pilgrimage to Lourdes. Last, Dave from Birmingham who had been touring Europe with his family joined us, but because of a ticketing error they had separated him from his family compartment.

It was a tight squeeze with five people and their luggage in a six-berth compartment, and having the spare middle bunk made it easier to manoeuvre. Dave and I stowed away the luggage for the ladies, and then we all settled down to our allocated bunks. Albert and Dave were both on the bottom bunk so I asked them if they wanted to swop with the top bunk. Albert looked shocked that I had even asked, then Dave volunteered. Not long after leaving the outskirts of the Austrian capital we all settled down and had a nice chat about where we had been and where we were going and by the time, we had passed Linz, everyone was asleep.

Morpheus and the smooth rocking of the OBB train had sent me into a very deep sleep, but it never lasted long. The train came to a halt at Wels in upper Austria then I felt someone tapping me on the shoulder. As I opened my eyes and pulled out my earphones I was looking up at a very tall white-haired old woman. She was standing above me shouting something in Austrian and pointing to the empty middle bunk. I thought what in god's name is she on about I was in Dave's bunk so I cannot be in the wrong one. Albert woke up, and he spoke good English so he translated the old dears rant for me. She had specifically booked a bottom bunk because of her age. Well, I could not argue with that so I got up and moved all my personal belongings to the middle bunk and asked Morpheus to send me back to sleep again.

The train had pulled into Passau on the German border

with Austria and the Police had come on board to check passports. I found this bewildering because we were in a Schengen area. I had my passport checked on boarding the train so actually checking passports at border crossing points in a Schengen area was illegal according to the European Council. Moreover, there had been no passport checks on leaving Munich because the train operator had checked them.

During my time in the Army I had been woken up many times by someone shining a torch in my face and it was not something I liked. So, when the German Federal Police officer shone his in my face, he was lucky I never swung for him. I had no problem with the checks it was just the sheer aggressive way they did it.

The Police officer asked what Stadt I was from I replied 'Nein Deutschland, Ich bin Schottlander', I then heard his partner say something like 'check the Englander' I just stared straight at him and he knew I understood exactly what he said. The officer then asked to see the passports of all those who were not German. It was all over in minutes, yet the way they did it was shocking.

I had been all over eastern Europe and had my passport checked many times and everyone had been courteous, and most of them knocked on the compartment door and introduced themselves. Here I was in Germany the architect of the free moving European Union getting treated like an illegal immigrant. It was not the German attitude I remembered from my service days and other trips. I guess the German immigration problem has taken its toll and the Police have become more robust in their approach. Anyway, by now, I was exhausted and the passive aggressive treatment from the Austrian woman and the Police was trying my patience. Home was beckoning me!

After Passau I settled down again, the compartment was now full and everyone was asleep. Then my sleep was interrupted again when we stopped in Nurnberg. This time it was a rather drunk German guy trying to get into the compartment. Luckily, I had put the chain guard on so he could only peek in and he was very lucky he never got a poke in the eye. The NightJet was becoming a nightmare. However, we only had five more stops to Cologne.

I woke up as the train pulled into Mainz, and the train steward was passing out breakfast. By this stage, there was only Dave, the old Austrian woman, and I left in the compartment. Chudy and Lou had got off at Frankfurt to get their connection to Lourdes and Albert was getting off at Mainz. The old Austrian woman signalled to me to tuck the bunks away and turn the compartment back to seating. By god, she was very stern looking and never smiled or even said thanks! I sat and chatted with Dave during breakfast then he went of re-join his family. I was now left with the old lady, but we were nearly at Koblenz so I just sat gazing out of the window as we passed the Rhine. As the train went through the Mosel valley, it took me back to my time in the Army and my travels through Wiesbaden, Baden-Baden and Karlsruhe, and it brought back an old ambition of wanting to cycle down the Rhine. Something I would like to do in the future.

The train stopped in Cologne, and it was my time to get off and leave the old woman to an empty compartment. As I left, I said 'Auf wiedersehen' to her, and she actually smiled and acknowledged my greeting.

Now I was looking forward to getting my connection to Brussels, in my mind my trip was over and I was now going home rather than exploring. I only had one hour to kill at the station. I found a Café in the shadow of Cologne Cathedral and ordered a coffee. I went through all my paperwork checking my Eurostar reservation and making sure I had everything I needed to get home.

As the time drew closer to my departure, I headed into Cologne Hauptbanhoff to look for my platform. The departure boards on platform 19 stated the Inter City Europe (ICE) train was scheduled to leave Cologne at 09.43am and arrive in Brussels at 11.35am, which gave me one hour and seventeen minutes to get through passport control at the Eurostar Terminal.

Not long after I got on the platform it came over the tannoy that the ICE 214 was running late. Here I was in one of the most important international railway hubs in Europe and my train was delayed. I thought to myself so much for Deutsche Bahn's reputation for punctuality. It was just like going to Vienna, as each minute passed my anxiety increased. Moreover, it was a Friday so my brain went into overdrive visualising the long queues at the Eurostar terminal. The situation was beyond my control so I just had to roll with it and hope for the best.

Finally, the ICE train turned up ten minutes late, which meant I only had a fifty-minute window to disembark the train, find the Eurostar terminal and get through passport control. However, like Vienna, there was no need for me to feel anxious or even worry about missing the Eurostar. The International Convention for the transportation of Passengers (CIV) insures all Interrail tickets. Therefore, all passengers with CIV tickets are assured onward transportation in the event of a cancelled or missed connection. You might even be compensated. So, one way or the other I would get home, it was just the embuggerance of it all and the thought of deviating from the plan at the last stage that irritated me.

So, the ICE train pulled into Brussels and I ran to the Eurostar terminal. It was busy, but because I had an Interrail ticket I had to go to a different ticket desk. Fortuitously, again having that ticket I avoided the long ticket queue and was fast tracked to passport control. In the end I got into the departure lounge with twenty minutes to spare. And, it was not long after that the call came over the tannoy telling everyone, to entrain.

As the Eurostar came out the other side of the Channel tunnel it was raining. I was in shorts and a t-shirt I had forgot to check the UK weather before leaving Brussels.

In the nine days I had been away, I had only seen rain once. Thus, the drop-in temperature hit me right away, it was a kind of welcome home, my journey was over!

Karlskirche Church, Vienna

EPILOGUE

I estimated I had travelled approximately 4,734 kilometers in nine days. That is the equivalent of going from Land's End to John O'Groats three times or doing half of the Trans-Siberian railway route. It was not a feat of endurance or exceptional; it was just different and very interesting.

A few days after I got back to London, I felt exhausted. It was the same feeling you get after a long-haul flight. I had never heard of anyone talk about having train lag. Maybe, it was one of those conditions that disappeared when people stopped using trains and started using budget airlines. But I wondered if such a condition in fact existed. The urban dictionary definition describes it as 'the feeling the rider will experience from the motion of a train' or 'taking a train that originates in night-time hours and ends in daylight'. Also, it has a lot to do with being shaken for a long time and the body returning to normal. I could not find any medical definition to substantiate it. However, I calculated that I had been away for approximately 216 hours and had been on a train for 76 hours of them so that is a long time to be shaken.

Apart from feeling tired, I was walking around on a high. I had a feeling of accomplishment as I had completed what I set out to do with no problem. I had crossed the Great Hungarian plain; saw its marshlands, floodplain, and steppe, even though I was asleep for most of it. I had taken a bath in a 16th, century Ottoman thermal spa. I had travelled through the medieval landscape of Transylvania and had crossed the iconic Bridge 889 into Bulgaria. I will not readily forget the trip through the Sićevo Gorge, and the walk along the old Iron Curtain. The beauty of Central Europe was outstanding, specifically the Pannonian plain and the sunflowers of Serbia. Most of all I had slept in the Hotel Moskva.

Historical wise I had visited some of the oldest cities on the globe and visited sites of significant political and of historical importance. They enlightened me in the brutality of the Communist rule at 60 Andrassy. I marvelled at the architectural influence of the Ottoman Empire in Bulgaria. Saw old traditions still being practiced such as the head nodding and admired the elegance of the Austro-Hungarian Empire in cities such as Zagreb. It has enhanced my knowledge of European history and how it was shaped through the centuries.

After years of stagnation living under the banner of communism, most of the countries in Central and southeast Europe in my point of view have become equals in one way or another. Since, the reforms of 1989 it has brought prosperity, better health care, and improved transport systems. Whilst in Slovakia I observed numerous tourists wandering about with bandages and eye patches because private healthcare is cheaper than in the affluent west. I went on a top of the range tram in Zagreb a lot more modern than a Croydon tram. I recall once reading an article in the Economist about the economy nearly collapsing in eastern Europe because they had been "on a binge fuelled by foreign investment [and] the desire for western living standards." That may be so, but they had learned a lesson, and got to grips with the European single market economy and are now on the rise. According to the European Commission Hungary, Romania, and Slovakia had the fastest growing economies in Europe during 2018.

However, difficulties still remain I saw crumbling train stations in Bulgaria and the struggling elderly woman and man in Zagreb. Nevertheless, there are similar difficulties in the west.

Politically in my assessment, the dissidence we saw back in the 1970s and 1980s is still simmering away under the facade of European populism. This was clear in the protests that had taken place in Bratislava before I went there and were about to happen again as I was leaving. The current generation of Slova-kians are searching for "truth" and "decency" against corruption in a democratic society and will use the legacy of 1989 to get it.

As for crime in the region, I encountered no hostility. The places I went to are as safe as any city in Europe. The people I came across were all helpful and frequently could not do enough for me. The receptionist in Sofia and the staff of the Kocmoc are prime examples. Admittedly, I felt uncertain at some stops along the way, but the existence of local Police soon put me at ease.

Interrailling, I absolutely recommend it. Apart from the expense of the reservations, it is an economical way to travel around Europe. I very much suggest the Global Pass, which provides you access to thirty countries. It will get you almost anywhere, and with the insurance of CIV you cannot go wrong. Some trains I travelled on were very outdated and poorly main-tained. However, that was all part of the adventure. Therefore, if you are looking to travel in style, the majority of the route I chose will not appeal to you. The weather got hot at times, so if you suffer from the heat do not travel in June or August. The lack of air con on most of the trains made it very uncomfortable at times.

Just like Joachim du Bellay's poem *Heureaux Qui, Comme Ulysses, au fait in beau voyage!* (Happy who, like Ulysses, made a beautiful trip!), it was a beautiful trip, and a great experience. It is one journey I will never forget!

ACKNOWLEDGMENTS

I had never ever thought about writing a book about a railway journey. After I returned to London, some friends encouraged me to record something. So, I have somewhat stumbled into the travelogue genre. But it is far from the likes of Bill Bryson or Paul Theroux.

The photos in the book were all taken by Phone. Photography is not a skill of mine, so please forgive the poor quality.

I would like to thank the following people for their inspiration, encouragement, and help in making this book possible. Rick Smith in South Africa for the inspiration to self-publish. An unnamed friend for the Hungarian tips and history. Lieutenant Colonel Don Wood, formerly Scots Guards who followed my journey, read my Facebook posts and encouraged me to write something. Candice Morton for looking at the many book covers and book titles and providing constructive feedback. Milena Daynova from Bulgarian National Radio for clarifying the issue of using the photo of the 'Unveiling of the Danube Bridge'. My old friend and author Nigel 'Spud' Ely, formerly 22nd Special Air Service Regiment for his encouragement, Amazon and Facebook marketing knowledge and suggestions. Also, I would like to thank all my friends on Social Media sites that followed my journey and commented on my posts it was very encouraging. Also, to my partner Dr Juanita Hoe for verbal editing, providing creative writing suggestions, and for pushing me to get it checked and rechecked. Lastly, but not least my old friend the Zulu War historian and former Scots Guardsman Cameron Simpson, he did the final edit!

If I have missed anyone else, please forgive me it was not intentional – I hope you enjoy the book!

Kevin Gorman

London 28/01/2019

JUST THE TICKET

ABOUT THE AUTHOR

Kevin Gorman was born in Bellshill, North Lanarkshire, and grew up in Glasgow. At the age of 16 he joined the Scots Guards and served for 25 years. He read history at Birkbeck College, University of London and Intelligence and Security Studies at Brunel, London University, and currently works in the City of London for a Global professional services firm.

Printed in Great Britain
by Amazon

86920656R00120